C000004220

present

Familyman

by Rikki Beadle-Blair

First performed at Theatre Royal Stratford East
Friday 2nd May 2008

Theatre Royal Stratford East
Gerry Raffles Square
Stratford
London
E15 1BN

www.stratfordeast.com

Familyman
by Rikki Beadle-Blair

Cast in order of appearance

Caesar	**Gary Beadle**
Deanna	**Jo Castleton**
Nelson	**Ricci McLeod**
Che	**Aaron Taylor**
Keisha	**Ayesha Antoine**
Evita	**Jo Martin**
Precious/Nana Grace	**Llewella Gideon**

Creative Team

Writer	**Rikki Beadle-Blair**
Director	**Dawn Reid**
Designer	**Nick Barnes**
Lighting Designer	**Mark Doubleday**
Sound Designer	**James Tebb for Thames Audio**
Music Producer	**Excalibah**

Theatre Royal Stratford East from 2nd May to 31st May 2008

An interview with Rikki Beadle-Blair the writer of *Familyman*

Rikki Beadle-Blair is a British actor, director, screenwriter, playwright, singer, aerobics teacher, designer, choreographer/dancer and songwriter of West Indian origin. He was first introduced to Theatre Royal's Stratford audiences as writer and director of the critically acclaimed drama *Bashment* in 2005.

Tell us a bit about Rikki Beadle-Blair.

I think the reason I create, is down to two things – My family – particularly my mother, who taught me to read very young, and my schooling in Bermondsey. I went to an experimental free school in the 70's, where I could study whatever I wanted in any manner I wanted. I used to put on plays all the time and make little films. It liberated me. I can write a script almost anywhere at anytime, quickly, freely and fearlessly – I can create entire productions out of scraps on the spot and never run out of ideas for the next one. I'm inspired constantly by everything and everyone. Free School gave me that. My schoolfriends gave me inspiration, my mother gave me resilience and independence, my brothers and sisters gave me my sense of humor and my adult friends (most of which I've had since I was young) continue to give me perspective.

How long have you been writing and what inspired you to write?

I can't remember a time when I wasn't writing. Reading and writing came almost in tandem with speaking. I've always loved words. There's both adventure and security in communication.

What would you consider your most significant work so far and why?

I don't know if I'm capable of writing anything that's not significant to me. Comedy or drama, there has to be something that challenges me in it. I have to look at things that perplex me and find my humanity in them. Our common thread. I guess my most significant work will be my next one. My next growth spurt.

What inspired you to write Familyman and why do you think it necessary to present this piece now?

I usually write plays with a cast in mind and let them inspire me. In this case, I started with the director in mind – she was my inspiration. Dawn and I had some wonderful exhilarating conversations and found our common ground,

3

our shared passion about family and parenting and youth. So, I wrote this play specifically for her. I always had Gary in mind for the role of Caesar, I could hear his voice in every word I wrote. Also, I have young people in my life that I've kind of adopted, and I struggle to balance being responsible for their guidance with my duty to encourage them to outgrow me and move on. I have issues with letting go of those I love. That's all in the play.

Is Familyman in any way a reflection of your story?

Yes, I am Caesar! And Nelson and Deanna and Evita and Precious.... I am all the characters. They are splinters of me, in passionate debate with one another – thrashing out the meaning of everything, trying to make sense of myself (or is that myselves?) Trying to make peace.

What do you hope that the audience will take away from the piece?

I hope that they will look at each other with less judgement and greater empathy and understanding. I hope they will review their own attitudes to family and friendship. That on the way home they will debate teen pregnancy and corporal punishment and parental responsibilities. But most of all I hope they'll be entertained and get value for money! In the end it's an evening out. I hope it will be one to remember.

Tell us a little about your relationship with Theatre Royal Stratford East and why you have returned to work here?

I love this theatre. I'm so honoured to have had even one play on here, let alone two! I wish I could do a play here every year. The atmosphere is unlike any other theatre I've worked in.

Do you think Theatre Royal Stratford has anything to teach the wider London theatre body?

Stratford East is an inspiration, its outreach programming, its connection with young audiences – its tackling of hot issues – who else would have staged a play like Bashment (2005)? Its sense of history and its sense of the future...unique. And Kerry Michael (Theatre Royal Stratford East's Artistic Director) has no boundaries regarding genre or target audiences. It's all about vision.

What has the reception to your work been like from the 'famous' Stratford audiences and is the East London audience different to elsewhere?

Well, they're noisy! It's the nearest I've come to experiencing what theatre-going must have been like at Shakespeare's Globe. The Stratford East audience is part of the play, and I bear that in mind when I write for this theatre. That kind of honesty of response – it's thrilling.

4

What's next for Rikki Beadle-Blair?

I am working on a set of new plays that I am very excited about. They'll be previewing at the Tristan Bates Theatre in Covent Garden on the second week of June – one, called *Screwface* is about a play being staged in a youth offenders unit, and another, *Touchy*, is about the life for gay people in Iraq... I've got a ton of plays looking for homes... I'm an orphanage filled with growing ideas that are looking for love.

Is there anyone in particular you'd like to thank?

I'd like to say a huge that you to: Joni, Johnny, Simon, Monica, Carleen, Gary, Tanya, Louis-Rae, Cassius, Carola, Buster, Nia, Sasha, Tameka, Ricky, Ninia, Darren, Duncan, Joel, Davie, Jenny, Arnie, Joe, Luke, Jason, Nathan, Anthony, Ludvig, Elliott, Giuseppe, Ashmeed, Fola, Altan, Becky, Antoine, Amsalan, Kerry, Dawn, everyone at Stratford East, The Staff of the Actor's Centre, The Tristan Bates Theatre and all at Team Angelica.

An Interview with Dawn Reid the Director of *Familyman*

Associate Director at Theatre Stratford East for the past four years Dawn Reid is well known for her dynamic energy. Her wide body of work includes *Funny Black Women on the Ed*ge and the recent Barbican transfer *The Harder They Come*. Dawn is also artistic coordinator for the Theatre's second space – Theatre Royal Bar.

Tell us a bit about Dawn Reid, what inspired you to get into directing and what brought you to Stratford East?

I have always been interested in theatre, in my school days I would never miss a drama lesson, and my teacher was a huge inspiration to me and became a great friend. Without realising it, theatre was to become a great part of my life. My parents are Jamaican and although born here, my culture is integral to me and my family, who I continually learn from, and who are an amazing support system. Directing was a gradual process for me, as I had started out acting first, then through working here at the Theatre I was able to further the interest I had gained. I have had a long association with Theatre Royal, from watching my first show and interviewing the cast members for a school exam, to working in the box office (when it lived under the main stairs), through to marketing, outreach and working with a company called The Posse. To eventually casting, producing, assisting directing and then my first show *Funny Black Women On The Edge*.

Tell us about Familyman from the director's perspective. What do you see are the key points and issues?

Familyman is a universal story that I think touches many issues that families have to deal with – from what good parenting is, to attitudes to teenage pregnancy and where your thoughts lie around discipline in your home.

What do you hope that the audience will take away from the piece?

I hope that the show will give audiences the opportunity to reflect and discuss the issues in the play, and just how essential being able to talk and listen to one another is.

Tell us about your relationship with Rikki Beadle-Blair and his writing.

I first met Rikki, when he wrote *Bashment*, which was produced here in 2005 and of course I had seen some of his work before. I love that his

6

writing doesn't hold back and he isn't afraid to deal with subjects that many would not dare to discuss. I really respect what he has to say, and how he uses theatre to do so, and was thrilled to bits, when he said yes to writing *Familyman*. I knew that we would work well together as a team.

What do you see as Stratford East's vision and how is this piece representative of that?

Theatre Royal Stratford East offers an opportunity to see fresh, new work that is diverse in both its performances and its audiences. *Familyman* is new writing that tackles issues that our local community faces, just like all the work we do. It allows a voice to be present on stage that may not always have an opportunity to do so and that has always been the strength of Theatre Royal Stratford East.

Cast in order of appearance

Gary Beadle

Gary Beadle's Theatre credits include: *Top Dog Under Dog* (Sheffield Crucible), *The Memory of Water* (Watford Palace Theatre), *Generations of the dead in the abyss of Coney Island Madness* (Contact Theatre), *Ticker tape and V Signs* (7:84 Theatre Co), *Welcome Home Jacko* (BTC New York), *Moby Dick* (Royal Exchange Manchester), *God's Second In Command* (Royal Court), *Alterations* (Stratford East), *Club Mix* (Riverside Studios), *Black Poppies* (National Studio). Television credits include: *Thieves are us, Doctors, Kerrching, Little Britain, Holby City, Eastenders, Casualty, Absolutely Fabulous, Born to Run, Honeymoon, Radical Chambers, QPR, Askey is Dead, Screenplay, Making Out, Shall I be Mother, Lenny Henry Show* and *Relative Strangers (*all BBC), *Family Affairs* (Pearson), *The Bill* (Thames), *Operation Good Guy* (Fugitive), *Thieftakers* (Carlton), *Glam Metal Detectives, G.L.C., Spaghetti Hoops, Les Dogs, Jealousy, The Crying game, Space Virgins from Planet Sex, Queen of the Wild Fronteer, Detectives on the edge of a nervous breakdown* (Comic Strip), *Murphy's Mob, Wail of the Banshee* (Central), *Just Like Mohicans* (Channel 4), *Club Mix, Big Mix, Saturday Action* (LWT), *Soap 18 – 30*, (Alomo), *I love Keith Allen*, (BSB), and *Paparazzo* (YTV). Film credits include: *Til Death Do Us Part, Wit, the Imitators, Driven – D.C.I., Memoirs of a survivor, Fords on Water, Absolute Beginners, Playing Away, Cresta Run* and *White Mischief*.

Jo Castleton

Jo trained at Middlesex University in Performing Arts. She recently finished playing Miriam in *Snake in the Grass* by Alan Ayckbourn at the Central Theatre Chatham and Wicked Witch in *Wizard of Oz* in Basingstoke. Other work includes a National Tour of *Cat on a Hot Tin Roof* playing Mae, *The Mystery Plays* for Bath Music Festival, *Taken In* by Rikki Beadle Blair at the Tristan Bates Theatre, Sally Driscoll in *Dangerous Obsession* and *Murder with Love* amongst other plays as part of Nottingham Theatre Royal's annual Thriller Season Company for the past 10 years, Yvonne in *Perfect Pitch* and Ruth in *Table Manners*, Voice Overs as Georgina Golightly in *Space 1889*, *The Tomorrow People* and *Sapphire and Steel*. Other theatre includes national tours of *The Magic Flute* playing Papagena, *Ghost Train*, *Hay Fever* as Jackie Coryton and *Sailor Beware* as Daphne Pink. At Liverpool Playhouse – Nancy in *Oliver Twist*, Mrs Cratchit in *Christmas Carol*, Carol in *Shakers*, Papagena in *The Magic Flute*, and Eve in the *Mystery Plays*. At Chester Gateway – Claudine in *Cinderella*, Mrs Dearly *101 Dalmatians* and Morgana Le Fay in *Merlin and Arthur*. TV and

Film includes *Cyberon* as Lauren Andersen, Abgail Clifford in *Doctors* (BBC), Natasha Alexander in *Auton2 Sentinel* and *Auton3 – Awakening* and Renee Duffy in *Duffy* (BBC).

Ricci McLeod

Rikki's theatre credits include: *Gone To Far, Catch* (both at the Royal Court Theatre) and *Two Step* (Almeida Theatre) Television credits include: *Holby Blue, Holby/Casualty Special, Doctors,* (All for the BBC), *Dub Plate Drama* (Red Mullett), *Ghost Squad* (Company Pictures), *Green Wings* (Tiger Aspect) and as series regular in 3 series of *William and Mary* (Granada Television). Film credits include: *Incendiary* (Film 4), *7Seven Lives* (Starfish Films) and *The Football Factory* (Vertigo Films.) Radio credits include: *Avoid London* for BBC Radio.

Aaron Taylor

Aaron Trained at The Harris Theatre School, Anna Scher, Tricyle and the BAC. Theatre credits include: *Grope Box* and *Taken In* (Team Angelica), *Measure for Measure* (Arcola), *Boy Soldier* (Tricycle), and *Elsewhere* (Kings Head). Television Credits include: *Sharman* (Carlton Television). Film Credits Include: *Souljah* (Team Angelica), *Kill Your Television* (One Song Productions), *The Red And The Black* (SOS Film), *Minute Man* (Eleventh Hour Productions) and *X-ed* (Tricycle).

Ayesha Antoine

Ayesha's theatre credits include: *Big White Fog* (Almeida Theatre directed by Michael Attenborough), *Master Juba* (Theatre Is/G.L.Y.P.T.), *Upstairs in the Sky* (Quicksilver), *The Firework Makers Daughter* (Hammersmith Lyric Theatre). Television credits include: *Dr Who, Holby City, Grange Hill* (BBC), *Kerching* (CBBC) and *The Bill* (Talkback Thames). Film credits include: *Operation Gadgetman* for Hallmark/Disney. Radio credits include: *The Number 1 Ladies Detective Agency, Things to Do Before You Die, Father and Son, The Fountain Overflows* (Radio 4), *Hands, The Lysistrata Project, Hold My Breath* (BBC Radio 3) *Four Four – Straight Town, Much Ado About Nothing, Westway* (BBC World Service), *Pericles* (BBC Radio Scotland), *The Bessie Coleman Story* (BBC Radio Schools).

Jo Martin

Jo Martin's theatre credits include: *Noughts & Crosses* (RSC), *Dona Flor And Her Two Husbands* (Lyric Theatre Hammersmith), *Coyote On a Fence* (Royal Exchange, Manchester/Duchess Theatre), *Somewhere The Shadow* (Contact, Manchester), *Oroonoko* and *Don Carlos* (both RSC), *Ready or Not* and *Funny Black Women on the Edge* (director/performer – both at Theatre Royal Stratford East), *Victor* and *The Ladies and Pecong* (both at the Tricylce Theatre), *Meridian* (The Contact Theatre), *Job Rocking* (The Riverside Studios), *To Kill a Mocking Bird* (The Mermaid Theatre), *A Temporary Rupture* (The Cockpit / Croydon Warehouse & National Tour), *Beef No Chicken and Dog* (both at the Shaw Theatre), *Majic* (Royal Court Theatre), *Nobody's Back Yard* (Umoja Theatre Co.), *Eldorado* (Theatre Royal Stratford East Upstairs). Television credits include: *Stupid*, *Doctors*, *Kerching*, *The Crouches, 40 Acres and a Mule, Casualty, Supergirlie, Blouse and Skirt, The Real McCoy, Chef* (Series 3), *Birds of a Feather, Dodgems, The Brittas Empire,* (all BBC), *All About George, A&E* (Granada), *The Bill* (Thames), *Blackout* and *Club Mix* (Channel 4). Film credits include: *Batman Begins*, *The Intimidation Game* (Warner Bros Productions) *Dead Meat, I Love My Mum* (Intense Productions), *For Queen & Country* (Zenith), *The Godsend* (Funky Black Shorts). Radio credits include: *Silver Street* (semi regular), *School plays 3* and *Windrush* (all BBC), *Little Big Woman 2*, *Emerald green, Vent* and *Airport* (Radio 4). Jo won the BFM International Film Festival Best Actress Award 2001 for her role in *Dead Meat*. Jo's first full-length play, *Shoot 2 Win!* played at the Theatre Royal Stratford East. She has also appeared with the Comedy Store Players at the Comedy Store.

Llewella Gideon

Llewella's professional career began in 1989 as an original cast member and writer/performer in all 6 series of *The Real McCoy* for the BBC. She has appeared in *Murder Most Horrid*, 3 episodes of *Absolutely Fabulous*, *The Lenny Henry Show*, *Big Train*, *Porkpie*, *The Crouches, Nighty Night*, *Eastenders*, *Holby City* and *Casualty* amongst others and various children's programmes. Theatre credits include *Running Dream* (Albany Theatre), *Bitter and Twisted* (Black Theatre Co-operative), *Temporary Rupture* (BTC), *The Amen Corner*, *Blues Brother Soul Sisters* at the Bristol Old Vic and *The Sunshine Boys*. Film credits include: *For Queen and Country, Different Girls, Spiceworld – The Movie* and Lars Von Trier's *Manderlay*. Radio work includes *Clement doesn't Live Here, Lenny Henry Easter Show, Behind the Couch, The Airport* and *The Emerald Green Show* as wells a several radio dramas. Llewella is also the voice of Molly and Trix in *Bob the Builder*. As a writer, she has successfully adapted and her one-woman show: *The Little Big Woman*, into a book and then in her own sit-com on Radio 4 *The Little Big Woman Radio Show*, which ran into a successful sit-com for Radio 4 which ran for 3 series. Llewella has written for both radio and television including CBBC's *Kerching*, *Smell the Purple* and *Fruit Salad*; her first full length theatre piece was later adapted for Radio 4's afternoon play.

Creative Team

Rikki Beadle-Blair Writer

Born and raised in South London, Rikki attended Lois Acton's Experimental Bermondsey Lampost Free School. Rikki wrote his first play at the age of seven and began directing aged eleven. After a diverse career; that often spilled out of the world of fringe theatre to take in six months in a Baghdad Cabaret, performing in a snake act across the UK, and choreographing Brazilian strippers, Rikki co-founded the Rock Band 'Boysie', garnering a large following on the London gig circuit. Due to his cult work in the theatre Rikki was hired to write movie *Stonewall* for BBC and US indie film company, Killer Films. The movie, directed by Nigel Finch, went on to win the audience awards at the London Film Festival and the San Francisco Lesbian and Gay film festival as well an award for Rikki at Outfest LA for Outstanding Screenwriting. Among other television projects, Rikki wrote, directed and featured in the internationally successful Channel 4 series *Metrosexuality, also* composing the soundtrack. He has also worked extensively for BBC Radio 4, writing and performing his own series of plays. His documentary *Roots of Homophobia* won the Sony award for Best Radio Feature. His recent hugely successful production of *Bashment* at Theatre Royal Stratford East was nominated for Best New Play by the TMA. Rikki recently wrote and directed the Stage Adaptation of *Stonewall* at the Pleasance in Edinburgh and the Drill Hall Theatre – the cast was nominated for Best Ensemble in the 2007 Stage Awards. His most recent; *Fit* about teen sexuality has just completed a sell out tour (Birmingham Rep, Unity Liverpool, Glasgow CCA, etc) and played to schools in an outreach program all around the UK. (Birmingham Rep, Unity Liverpool, Glasgow CCA, etc) and played to schools in an outreach program all around the UK. His Theatre Company 'Team Angelica' has been resident at the Tristan Bates Theatre in Covent Garden which has hosted previews of his *South London Passion Plays* trilogy: *Gutted*, *Laters* and *Sweet* detailing the lives and loves of Bermondsey rudeboys. Other plays developed there include *Taken In*, (set in halfway house for homeless youths), *Totally Practically Naked in My Bedroom on a Wednesday Night* (a teenage sex farce), *Move* (set at the time of Soho bombings), *Below the Radar* set in the boho community and *Human* in which a love affair between two people with only nine months to live, was acted by a different couple every night portraying characters of widely varying races, sexes, sexualities and social backgrounds. Rikki's other recent work includes writing and directing *Juicy* at the Contact Theatre Manchester. Composing and directing the musical *Prettyboy* at Oval House Theatre, where he also directed Matt Harris's *Venom,* writing *Gunplay* for Big Fish Theatre Company. And writing and directing *Ask & Tell* at the Soho Theatre for the NYT. He was a writer and the executive story editor for the US TV series, *Noah's Arc*, and was supervising director of debut films with first-time Filmmakers as a director for the *Out in Africa* organization in South Africa. Rikki had just directed the short film *Soulijah* by John Gordon about a gay former child soldier living in South London, which premiered at the London Film Festival and is currently touring film festivals. He has also directed

Best Man by Greg Owen and Nick McGarrigle, which is opening this month at The New Theatre, Dublin. Work Rikki is developing with new writers includes Jai Rajani's *onenite.com*, about asian boys and internet sex), *Johnny Rice* by Bronya Deutsch (a children's play), John Gordon's *Fagamuffin* (a gay yardie romance) and 15-year-old Paul Jaramenko's *Forced* (about teen delinquency).

Rikki's new projects previewing this June are *Screwface*, about a drama workshop in a young offenders unit, and *Touched*, about gay life in Iraq. Also *Now You See It* written for a predominantly disabled cast. Rikki loves to work with new and interesting actors and writers – you can contact him on rikkibb@aol.com.

Dawn Reid Director

Dawn is the Associate Director at Theatre Royal Stratford East and her association with the theatre has included assisting on shows such as *One Dance Will Do*, *Aeroplane Man, Windrush* and *Things Change*. Dawn has produced festivals for the theatre including *Gateway to the Arts*, a series of shows for and by young people, and *Spoke-Fest*, a two-week festival of spoken word, performances and workshops. Dawn has also produced Boy Blue's sold-out show *The Book of Koraka* and produced and directed *Club V*. Her directing credits for Theatre Royal Stratford East include *Funny Black Women on the Edge*, Ade Ikoli's *Diary of a SingleMan*, DRD's *Dis is How We Do It*, *Speechify: Four men on Family*, the Kat Francois one-woman show *Me, Myself and 7*, *Da Mic Sounds Nice*, *Summit* and *The Harder They Come* (also, recently transferred to the Barbican). Dawn was the Assistant Director on *Jack and the Beanstalk, Aladdin* and *Red Riding Hood*, and she directed *Sleeping Beauty* and *The Snow Queen*. She has also directed rehearsed readings for Brit Asia and New Voices, part of the theatre's work with new writers. Other theatre credits include directing Llewella Gideon's premiere of *Fruit Salad* (Greenwich Theatre) and working as Associate Director on *Avenue Q* (Noël Coward Theatre). Dawn is the co-creator of Spoke-Lab with Roger Robinson and the recipient of a Carlton Multicultural Achievement Award for Performing Arts.

Nick Barnes Designer

Nick studied drama at Hull University and theatre design at the Slade School of Fine Art. He has designed operas and musicals at home and abroad including *West Side Story* and *Showboat* (Austria), *Martin Guerre* (Denmark), *20,000 Leagues Under the Sea* (Theatre Royal Stratford East), *Miss Saigon* (Goteborgs Operan) and *Hansel and Gretel*, (Norwegian National Opera). In 1997 Nick co-founded Blind Summit Theatre, which aims to make cutting edge puppetry based theatre for adult audiences and for which he designs, makes puppets and performs. The company is making a name for itself performing nationally and internationally. Their Bukowski inspired show *Low Life* about puppets stuck in a bar, which was part of the London International Mime Festival in January 2006 will this year be seen in America, Columbia, Germany, Spain and China. They also provided the puppets for the ENO's award winning production of Madame Butterfly directed by the late Anthony Minghella, which was also performed at The Metropolitan Opera, New York.

Mark Doubleday Lighting Designer

Mark has lit over 250 productions in most UK Theatres and also New York, Washington, Europe and Asia. Mark's recent work includes: *Behzti* at Birmingham Rep, *Lysistrata* at Houston Grand Opera/New York City Opera, *Hansel & Gretel* at Scottish Opera, *Love's Labour's Lost* at Washington DC Shakespeare Theatre and RSC. *Tannhäuser* (Los Angeles Opera), *Mikado* (Gielgud Theatre, London). Future engagements include: *Fast Labour*, (West Yorkshire Playhouse), *The Cumner Affair*, (Tête à Tête), *Tannhäuser*, (Teatro Real, Madrid), *Le Cantatrice Chauve*, (Athénée Théâtre, Paris).

James Tebb Sound Designer for Thames Audio

James studied for three years at the University of Hull, following which he put his degree course in biology to good use by starting a career in the music industry. Over the next six years he engineered and designed many shows and events for both live music and corporate clients, working with countless artists from all genres of music. After marrying into the wonderful world of theatre, James finally crossed the track from live music to enjoy an involvement in numerous theatre shows both in the UK and overseas. Over this period James forged an excellent relationship with Thames Audio whom he now works full time for designing sound systems for theatre, television and corporate events. Most recently James was sound designer for *Marilyn and Ella* here at Theatre Royal Stratford East.

Excalibah Music Producer

At the delicate and tender age of 18 Excalibah was plucked from relative obscurity (pirate radio) by the BBC and catapulted to lofty heights as the first signing to 1Xtra. As a DJ he is well known for promoting fresh UK talent and even filled in for the legendary John Peel. He has played music to rooms full of sweaty people all across the world and has been resident at London's biggest clubs; Fabric and Ministry of Sound as well as currently running his own night at Herbal in Shoreditch once a month. Radio credits include: Shows on BBC Radio 1, BBC Asian network, BBC 6Music, BBC 1Xtra. He also won 'Best Radio Show' and 'Best Radio Presenter' in the hip-hop press for 2003, 2004 and 2005. He can currently be heard worldwide on Pyroradio.com. Writing credits include: A monthly column for Hip Hop Connection and Big Smoke; Article for Sunday Telegraph, Knowledge, SOS and IDJ. Film & Theatre credits include: *Tube Tales, Aeroplane Man, Spoke Fest, 10 Poet Slam* and *Da Boyz* which he composed and musically directed; Jean Genet's *The Blacks* (Time Out *****) which he co-directed, composed and starred in. He has also written music for *Origin:Unknown*, *Medea* and *The Snow Queen* (all at Theatre Royal Stratford East). He composed and directed the short film *Cool Charm Corrected*, which won funding from the Hitchcock Foundation. Excalibah is currently working on projects for Theatre Royal Stratford East, Soho Theatre and the New London Orchestra. Lecturing and directing workshops and projects with Cardboard Citizens, Soho Theatre, Stratford East, Central School of Speech and Drama, Arts Council England and NAYT. He is the youngest member on the Board of Directors at Theatre Royal Stratford East.

THEATRE ROYAL
STRATFORD EAST

2007 LAURENCE OLIVIER AWARD WINNER

Production Credits

Wardrobe Supervisor – **Amita Kilumanga**

Scenic construction – **Steel the Scene**

Special thanks to: Upton Park Snooker Centre
Carphone Warehouse
London Mets Youth Baseball Club, Finsbury Park
Sunrise Bakery
MC Trooper
Skankz

Theatre Royal Stratford East Staff

Artistic Director	**Kerry Michael**
Executive Director	**Vanessa Stone**

Artistic

Associate Director	**Dawn Reid**
Resident Director	**Mathilde Lopez**
Associate Producer	**Karen Fisher**
Project Manager, IFEA	**Annette Telesford**
Assistant To Artistic Director	**Katja Janus**
Associate Artists	**Poonam Brah, Fred Carl (US), Clint Dyer, Robert Lee (US), Ryan Romain, Ultz**
Theatre Archivist	**Murray Melvin**
Assistant Archivist	**Mary Ling**

Administration

Theatre Manager	**Graeme Bright**
Administration Assistant	**Velma Fontaine**
Development Director	**Elizabeth Royston**
Development Officer	**Karen Richardson**
Head of Finance	**Paul Canova**
Finance Officers	**Titilayo Onanuga & Elinor Jones**

Youth Arts & Education

Head of Youth Arts & Education	**Jan Sharkey-Dodds**
Project Manager	**Serena B. Robins**
Youth Arts Officer	**Karlos Coleman**
Hear My Voice Coordinator	**Ryan Romain**

Marketing And Press

Head of Marketing & Sales	**Barry Burke**
Press & Marketing Officer	**Lynn Patrice Ochoa**
Marketing Assistant	**Samuel Bawden**
Box Office Operations & Sales Manager	**Praveen Sond**
Box Office Manager	**Beryl Warner**
Box Office Supervisor	**Angela Frost**
Box Office Assistants	**Ana Gizelda Burke, Asha Bhatti, Asha Jennings-Grant, Kemisha Plummer, Monika Maslanka, Sharleen Fulgence**

Production

Production Manager	**Kate Edwards**
Company & Stage Manager	**Sarah Buik**
Deputy Stage Manager	**Lorna Adamson**
Assistant Stage Manager	**Natasha Gooden**
Chief Electrician	**Dave Karley**
Deputy Chief Electrician	**Kyle Macpherson**
Wardrobe Manager	**Korinna Roeding**

Technical Resources

Resources & Technical Manager	**Stuart Saunders**

Front Of House

Senior Duty Manager	**Liz Okinda**
Duty Managers	**Rameeka Parvez & Nana Agyei**
Ushers	**Akosua Acheampong, Alesha Williams, Avita Jay, Billy Walton, Catherine Philips, Charles Leanson, Danai Mavunga, Denise Blake, Heather Walker, Jalil Saheeb, Jenine Marie Nelson, Joan Kagunza, Leon Lynch, Magdalena Sobczynska, Michaela Collins, Miria Kyamanywa, Richard Skeete, Sade Olokodana, Sakaa Mensah, Sarpong Mensah, Sharee Zvye, Shophie Bradley, Yemi Balogun**
Bar Supervisors	**Chris Crawford-Divine, Magdalena Molak, Nasrine Hasnaoui**
Bar Team Leaders	**Louise Brown, Ysanne Tidd**
Bar Assistants	**Adrian Pawlus, Agata Dziewiecka, Andrew Bazeley, Bethan Gailland Lynch, Charlene Pierre, Daniel Akogu Agudah, Desiree Brown, Estella Campbell, Gemma Neve, Giles Bursnell, Jason Hadley, Rose Marie, Shantimalar Christian**
Fire Marshals	**Kofi Agyemang-Prempeh, Liz Okinda, Rameeka Parvez**
Maintenance	**John Munday**
Domestic Assistants	**Ann Spearman, Helen Mepham, Julie Lee, Magdalena Sobczynska**

Board of Directors

Sally Banks, Bonnie Greer, Tony Hall (Chair), **Wasfi Kani, John Lock, Jo Martin, Murray Melvin** (Company Secretary), **John Newbigin, Paul O'Leary, Shannen Owen, Mark Pritchard, Sarah Isted** (Treasurer), **Matthew Xia**

THEATRE ROYAL
— STRATFORD EAST —

2007 LAURENCE OLIVIER AWARD WINNER

Contacting the Theatre

Theatre Royal Stratford East
Gerry Raffles Square
Stratford
London
E15 1BN

e-mail theatreroyal@stratfordeast.com
Website www.stratfordeast.com

Tickets and Information 020 8534 0310
Administration 020 8534 7374
Fax 020 8534 8381
We are delighted to take Typetalk calls for
deaf people or if you prefer send us a text
07972 918 050
Press Direct Line 020 8279 1123
Education Direct Line 020 8279 1107

Offices open	Mon – Fri	10am – 6pm
Box Office open	Mon – Sat	10am – 7pm
Bar open	Mon – Sat	11am – 11pm
	Sunday	12am – 10.30pm
Food served	Monday	12.30pm – 9.30pm
	Tues – Sat	12.30pm – 8.30pm
	Sun	1pm – 8pm

Caribbean Flavours in the Theatre Royal Bar

The finest fish and chicken spiced and cooked to perfection by our chef,
Wills, as well as a wide range of non-Caribbean food, salads and snacks.
Now available in the Theatre Royal Bar. For further information, please ring:
02082791163

Thanks to the supporters of the Theatre Royal

We thank the core supporters of Theatre Royal Stratford East: Arts Council
England, London Borough of Newham and London Councils.

We would also like to say thank you for the support from: Esmée Fairbairn
Trust, Jack Petchey Foundation, European Social Fund, Mercers' Company,
The Big Lottery Fund, PRS Foundation, Heritage Lottery Fund, Football
Foundation, King Baudouin Foundation, Calouste Gulbenkian Foundation,
Connecting Communities Plus (DCLG), Harold Hyam Wingate Foundation,
Garfield Weston Foundation, Grange Park Opera Company, Moneygram, Comic
Relief, Mackintosh Foundation, John Ellerman Foundation, Rayne Foundation,
D'Oyly Carte Charitable Trust.

Birkbeck and Theatre Royal Stratford East

A great new cultural and educational partnership for east London. Birkbeck and Theatre Royal Stratford East believe that it is central to their aims and philosophy to play a leading role in the development of the cultural and social life of east London. Both organisations seek to offer a wide range of individuals the opportunity to develop their potential and enhance their lives, and are delighted to be working in partnership to deliver these outcomes.
Birkbeck, University of London. London's specialist provider of part-time evening university courses now in Stratford. Top qualifications from the University of London. Generous financial support and bursaries. For more information visit www.birkbeckstratford.ac.uk

Vision Collective

With Thanks To The Ongoing Support From Our Vision Collective Members
Anonymous, Brenda Blethyn, Jim Broadbent, Derek Brown, The Avis Bunnage Estate, Bonnie Greer, Tony Hall, Laurence Harbottle, Philip Hedley CBE, David Hutchins, Jeremy Irons, Michael Lynas, Sofie Cooper Mason *(Offwestend. com)*, **Ian McKellen, Murray Melvin, Oberon Books Ltd, Shannen Owen, Derek Paget, Toni Palmer, Neil Pearson, Jon Potts, Alan Plater & Shirley Rubinstein, Eleni & Costas Sakellarios, Hedley G Wright**

Would you like to become a member of the Vision Collective and help secure the future of Theatre Royal? Membership starts at £500 per year and gives you a rare opportunity to align yourself with the development of future productions. As a Vision Collective member, you will receive an invitation to a Vision Collective receception with the artistic director and cast on the first night of the productions you support as well as invites to 'meet and greet' the cast and crew, opportunities to attend rehearsals and other benefits.
For more information, contact Kerry Michael on 020 8279 1100 or email kmichael@stratfordeast.com.

FAMILYMAN

For Tanya

First published in 2008 by Oberon Books Ltd
521 Caledonian Road, London N7 9RH
Tel: 020 7607 3637 / Fax: 020 7607 3629
e-mail: info@oberonbooks.com
www.oberonbooks.com

A catalogue record for this book is available from the British
Library.

ISBN: 978-1-84002-858-4

Cover design by Luke Wakeman

Printed in Great Britain by CPI Antony Rowe, Chippenham.

Characters

CAESAR – 34 Black

DEANNA – 34 White

NELSON – 17 Mixed-race

KEISHA – 17 Black

CHE – 17 Any race

EVITA – 31 Black

PRECIOUS – 51 black

NANA GRACE – 60s black

Spot up on CAESAR.

CAESAR: He's dead.

Spot up on DEANNA.

DEANNA: Caesar. Breathe.

CAESAR: I'm telling you, Deanna. He's dead. End of. Deal with it. He's dead.

DEANNA: He's seventeen.

CAESAR: Was.

DEANNA: He's your son.

CAESAR: Was my son. And now he's a dead man. Dead. Dead, dead.

DEANNA's phone rings. She goes to answer it. CAESAR holds his hand out. She gives it to him. He answers it.

You're dead.

He hangs up.

DEANNA: Caesar! He's seventeen!

CAESAR: And it's one am. On a Monday. Ain't Friday, ain't Saturday – ain't half-term – and you ain't his best friend or his counsellor or his spokesperson. You're his mum. And I'm his dad. And this is my house. And when he comes through my front door – He's dead.

DEANNA: Thanks to you.

CAESAR: Don't thank me, ma'am – it's my job.

DEANNA: Killing your kid?

CAESAR: Oh, here we go…

DEANNA: Just leaving him to die somewhere out there in the middle of the night? Is that your idea of being a dad?

CAESAR: Melodrama queen!!! What? He's dying somewhere in some gutter on the Mean Streets of Forest Gate? That's what he rang you on your mobile to say?

DEANNA: I dunno. I never answered it.

CAESAR: Deanna – He's fine.

DEANNA: Is he?

CAESAR: He's fine!

DEANNA: Is that what he told you?

CAESAR: He's fine!!!

DEANNA's phone rings. CAESAR grabs it.

You alright?

THE RAMSAY HOME/DA CLUB

Loud music.

Spot on NELSON.

NELSON: Whaddup bruv!!

Music down to low level with phone filter effect.

CAESAR: Bruv?

Music goes up for NELSON's moments and back down to phone filter low level for CAESAR and DEANNA.

NELSON: Mate, man, dread, blood, geeezerrrrr!

CAESAR: What the fuck is that noise?

NELSON: Grime!

CAESAR: Crime?

NELSON: Grime bruv! Grrrrrrriiiiime!

CAESAR / DEANNA: He's drunk.

DEANNA: Speakerphone!

CAESAR snaps the phone to speaker.

NELSON waves the phone aloft as he dances...

NELSON: Grrrrrrrrrrriiiiiiiiiiiiiiimmmmme, bruv!!!!!

DEANNA: Nelson?

NELSON: (*Back to phone.*) Dad? Can you hear me? You still on, or you hung up? Whatever, man – sweet – I love you, Dad!

DEANNA: He what?

NELSON: I LOOVVE YOUUUU DAAAADDD!

DEANNA: Oh my God, he's on drugs!

DEANNA snatches the phone.

Nels! It's mummmy!

NELSON: Mummeeeeee! Mummy and Daddy! I love you Mummy and Daddy!

CAESAR: You fucking little crack-head! Where the fuck are you?

NELSON: Ooooohhhh! Daddy said Ef!

CAESAR: ...Dead.

DEANNA: Nelson, babe! Is Che there?

NELSON: Che!

Spot up on CHE.

CHE: Yo.

NELSON: (*Throwing phone.*) You here?

CHE: (*Catching phone.*) Don't get deep, man. You know I ain't a thinker. (*Into phone.*) Yo.

DEANNA: Che!

CHE: Who wants him?

DEANNA: It's Deanna…

CHE: Deanna?

DEANNA: Nelson's mum.

CHE: Oh, Dee!

CAESAR: 'Dee'?

CHE: Whassup, Deannaaaaa!!!?

CAESAR: CHE!

CHE: Shit!

He throws the phone back to NELSON.

NELSON: (*Into phone.*) Mum?

CAESAR: (*Grabbing DEANNA's phone.*) CHE!

NELSON: (*Tossing phone to CHE.*) It's for you.

CHE: Shit. (*Into phone.*) Mr Ramsay.

CAESAR: I'm gonna ask you this calmly – and I'm gonna ask you this once. Where the fuck are you?

CHE: At Da Klub.

CAESAR: 'Da Klub'?

CHE: Dee knows!

CAESAR looks at DEANNA.

CAESAR: Da Klub?

BAM!

A NEON SIGN READS: 'DA KLUB'

Music: Grime.

CAESAR and DEANNA make their way through the bouncing young crowd.

CAESAR: 'Da Klub'?

DEANNA: They're probably over by the stage.

CAESAR: 'Da Klub'? Why can't nobody spell no more? I tell you why – 'cause they're all up in 'Da Klub' on a school night instead of studying for their A levels and GCS… Je-sus!

CAESAR just avoids bumping into a sweaty GIRL DANCER.

Calm down darlin'. You'll pull something.

The GIRL DANCER throws her arms around him.

Not me! Careful, gyal, my wife'll have your eyes out!

DEANNA is grabbed by a dancing CHE.

CHE: Dee!

DEANNA: Che!

CAESAR: Oy! Home-wrecker! She's taken! (*Staring at the grinding GIRL DANCER.*) I'm taken… We're… Lord Jesus Chris'ave mercy pon me…

CAESAR starts to grind with the GIRL DANCER. Suddenly the music stops…and there is NELSON.

NELSON: Dad?

CAESAR: Er, hello, son?

The music kicks back in blurry and echoey, as NELSON throws his arms round CAESAR.

NELSON: Dad!

CAESAR hugs his son for a moment.

CAESAR: Damn fool…

CAESAR pushes NELSON off, smacks him round the head and starts to check his eyes. NELSON smiles.

NELSON: Daddyyyyy…

NELSON spots DEANNA, who is dancing up a storm…

Mummyyyy!

…and lunges across to hug his mother, segueing straight into a grind.

CAESAR: Okay, Oedipussy, break it up! Let's go! Last call for the rehab express!

Music changes…

CHE: Yo, yo, yo, yo, yo, Nels, Nels, Nels, man! It's on!

DJ: It's offi-ci-aaaal! Proof that grime does pay! Tonight's purse is t'ree hundred poun'! In the white corner the revolutionary of rhyme – MC Che!

The crowd parts to reveal that CHE and NELSON are holding mics…

…and in the brown corner – the Warrior of words! MC Nelson! Bus' it!

CHE: *Check, Check, Check*
See the place get wrecked wrecked wrecked
The beat's set to bruk bruk your neck
If a soldier don't come come correck!
See, I got more rhymes than you got asbos
I got more rhymes than your pimp got clothes,
I got more rhymes, more riddims more flows
I forgot more rhymes than you ever gonna know.
See you cruising round your lowly Ends
In your low-spec jacked Mercedes Benz
Trying to Mack like you got serious spends

> *Like your ride might finally get you friends*
> *Likkle swordfish that thinks that he's a shark,*
> *he might be King Don down in Upton Park,*
> *But this is my manor, chief, n'you been marked,*
> *And King Donnie he's gonna get darked!*

The crowd cheers – they're feelin' it!

DEANNA: Whooooo!

She looks at stone-faced CAESAR.

You still alive or is this rigor mortis?

CAESAR: You wanna be careful jumping up and down like that at your age, something might fall off.

NELSON: *Check-check, Check, Check!*
> *Do I detect four walls that stand erect?*
> *Did I take your words out of context?*
> *I thought the place was set to get wrecked?*
> *Your dictionary needs a wee updater*
> *You're looking at a true force of nature*
> *The definition of rhyme annihilator*
> *You jus' an Anakin, this here's Darth Vader,*
> *'Cause the lyrical Infiltrator reach*
> *Word tsunami tearing up the beach*
> *Hear the lexical instigator teach*
> *Vocabulary like scripture hear me preach*
> *Tune your radio to station after station,*
> *Hear my voice in every corner of the nation*
> *I am essential like sex – I'm procreation*
> *I'm mass media, you're masturbation!*
> *Flex!*

The crowd goes wild, indicating he's the winner.

DEANNA: Oh my God! He's amazing!

CAESAR: (*Busily texting.*) Remind me to pat him on the back later.

DEANNA: Caesar! That's your son burning up the mic!

CAESAR: On a school night.

DEANNA: Caesar, he's killing 'em!

CAESAR: On a school night.

DEANNA: Oh my gosh, man! Who the hell are you?

CAESAR: I'm a dad.

DEANNA: Dad or granddad? When did you get so old? How did you forget your youth so quickly? We met on a school night. Weren't that long ago you were spitting lyrics and drunk as a skunk and seventeen and sexy as hell and I was snatched at first sight – we used to know how to have fun!

CAESAR: And then you got pregnant and youth was over. And fun was a memory. Like I said – I'm a dad. And you're a mother, Sweaty Betty.

DJ: Can no-one challenge this brother? Who's got the skills to depose the Don? Ain't no Napoleon got the minerals to take Nelson's bones apart?

DEANNA grabs CAESAR's hand and pulls it up in the air!

DEANNA: Yo!

CAESAR: (*Yanking his hand down.*) Whoa!

DEANNA grabs the mic.

DEANNA: Introducing the original Black Caesar – Emperor of Grime, Dictator of Rhyme – Bow down, Admirable Nelson, and meet your Waterlooo!!!

NELSON circles CAESAR, who stands, arms folded.

NELSON: *Yo, yo, what's that sound*
Everybody check what's coming down

  Yo, yo what do you know
  It's chucking out time
  At the old folk's home
  It's rainin' it pourin'
  The Old man is borin'

CHE: *I can't stan' da Raiiiiin!!!*

NELSON: *That ain't the rain*
  On the window pane
  It's the tap-tap-tap
  Of the old man's cane
  The clack-clack-clack
  Of the Zimmer frame –

CHE: *Zim Zimmer!*

NELSON: *It's your meals on wheels dinner!*
  I'll be your ambulance driver
  Let me wipe off some of that saliva
  Question!
  You have indigestion?
  How come your belly gettin' bigger
  And your legs gettin' thinner?
  Shall I cut your steak finer?
  Or just chuck it in the liquidiser?
  Don't sweat it, Pater –
  Drink up your Dinner we'll find your teeth later
  Sorry pops –
  Do you need me to stop?
  Am I chattin' too fast for your hearing aid?
  Am I making you choke on your Lucozade?
  Does my youthful dexterity 'n' energy faze ya?
  That's 'cause I'm here to bury Caesar not praise ya!

 The CROWD cheers. CAESAR grabs the mic.

CAESAR: Drop it!

Old skool beat – CAESAR bobs his head.

What you hear is not a test,
I'm a-rapping to the beat.
Ain't garage, ain't grime,
It scans and it rhymes
And I'm taking it to the street

I'm talkin' bout
Old Skool…
This groove is Old Skool
I ain't sayin' that old's cool
But I ain't gonna lie

I'm bringing you
Old Skool
I ain't lookin to scold you
But this flow will fold you
'Cause this riddim is fly

'Cause my name is Caesar R
And I'd like to say hello
To all you sucker MCs
With your wickety-wack beats
And your jacked-up jack-off flows

Word to the Mother,
Yo, mister lover-lover
Crapping mics 'bout your fertility
There's something you should know,
Yo, baby Romeo
Making kids requires losing your virginity
Say
Hotel, Motel, what you gonna do today?
It ain't easy gettin' some,
When you're living with your Mum
And your Daddy makes your girl wanna stray
Everybody say

Hotel, Motel, Holiday Inn!
I wonder where you gonna run
When it's time to have your fun,
And you can't bring your babe to your crib?

Who's the Daddy?
Who's the Daddy?
Who's got the skillz that pay the billz?
Who's the Daddy?
Who's the Daddy?
Who's the Mack Papi that keeps it real?

Beat steps on it.

CAESAR: *DtotheAtotheD-D-Y!*
Raise the roof and touch the sky!
DtotheAtotheD-D-Y!
Hit 'em up, Throw 'em up, Toss 'em up, Keep 'em high!
…'Cause This is Riddim is Fly!…
Peace!

Beat stops on cue. Crowd goes mental. CAESAR *crosses his arms again.*

NELSON *snatches back the mic.*

NELSON: Beats!

Sorry Mister, Do I know you?
Who do reckon youre chatting to?
I know think that you got me sussed
But the lines you jus bus, them ridiculous
You don't know me!
Same last name…

NELSON / CHE: *You don't know me!*

NELSON: *Different game, blood!*

NELSON / CHE: *You don't know me!*

NELSON: *Same abode…*

NELSON / CHE: *You don't know me…*

NELSON: *Different code!*

> *There's more to being a Daddy*
> *Than DNA,*
> *There's more to modern parenting*
> *Than paying your way*
> *There's more to child-rearing*
> *Than sperm donation*
> *And doling out discipline*
> *I'll give you an illustration*
>
> *In seven months and eighteen days*
> *When my sweet lickle Gal from round the way*
> *Will make my seed bear fruit*
> *And we'll have a lickle yout*
> *Puberty, virginity,*
> *That's ancient history,*
> *Your boys all grown*
> *Yeah my oats are sown*
> *And my honie's oven's filled with my bun…*
> *So! Who's the Daddy now… Son?*

The music stops. CAESAR stares at his son darkly.

CAESAR: Oh. No. He. Didn't.

THE RAMSAY HOME

CAESAR: Oh. No. He. Did. 'Nt.

DEANNA: Cocoa, anyone? Hot chocolate, Nels, babes?

CAESAR: 'Hot chocolate'? (*Kissing teeth.*) Ain't you heard, woman? Your pickney's a man now. Skip the hot chocolate, break out the hard booze – and let's get rat-assed together! A toast! To Family Values!

DEANNA: Okay. You're upset.

CAESAR: Wow, you don't miss a thing do you, Doc?

DEANNA: You're shocked.

CAESAR: You see? Sharp as a tack!

DEANNA: I think you should sit down… I think we should all sit down and have some cocoa and talk about this…

CAESAR: I'm just an open book to you! Transparent in the piercing spotlight of your perception… FUCK YOUR COCOA!

CAESAR: Fuck talking about it! I'm a thirty-something with a seventeen-year-old kid I can't afford who's about to become a dad to a grandchild I definitely can't afford! I'm pissed off and I'm disappointed and I don't want to sit down, I don't want a calm reasonable conversation and I don't want cocoa! Fuck your cocoa! FUCK!! YOUR FUCKING!!! COCOA!!!!

Pause.

NELSON: There's no need to swear at her.

Pause. CAESAR looks at NELSON.

CAESAR: (*Very quietly.*) Excuse me?

NELSON: There's no need to swear at mum. It's not her fault.

CAESAR: Oh. Right. Not her fault. Her indulgent best friend act has had no bearing whatsoever on the fact that you're an out of control stupid dirty stop-out with balls for brains and a bun in some bint's oven.

NELSON: No. It ain't.

CAESAR: 'Course it ain't. It's Daddy the Disciplinarian's fault. Forced to rebel against the regime and struggling to slip the stranglehold of Papa's Nazi Noose, you lost your footing,

37

tripped and fell and landed on top of some 'sket', is that your story?

NELSON: She ain't a sket, Dad. Stop calling her names. You don't know her.

CAESAR: Do *you*? Where'd you meet this ghetto Madonna? Hanging out at the mall, drinking cider?

NELSON: I met her at sixth form college.

CAESAR: She's not a teacher is she?

NELSON: No.

CAESAR: T'ank you Jeezus! Dinner-lady?

NELSON: She's in my drama group.

CAESAR: How ironic.

DEANNA: Excuse me, but who's creating the drama now?

CAESAR: Excuse me, but who decided to announce he was siring a child on a bloody microphone to an entire nightclub? My son told me he was making the biggest mistake of his life in a bleedin' rap for Chrissake, and I'm the one creating drama? Why couldn't he just be gay or something?

DEANNA: Oh, yeah, you'd love that!

CAESAR: Okay, I wouldn't love it – but I'd hate it less. And it'd be a lot less of a surprise, great big mummy's boy that he is. Go on son, please be gay, a bit more discrimination won't kill you – but you're not ready for a kid. You're sure this girl is biologically female? She is actually pregnant is she and not just a tranny with wind and womb envy?

NELSON: Dad. She's female. Trust.

CAESAR: (*Looking at NELSON's eyes.*) And you think you're in love with her. I presume she's pretty? Sorry, I'm old... 'Fit'?

NELSON: Oh my dayz, man…fit don't cut it.

CAESAR: Fit never does.

NELSON: Chung.

CAESAR: I thought we weren't swearing?

NELSON: She's well chung. Beyond sexy, beyond lush. She's Boom ting.

CAESAR: Well, that's settled. And her Intelligence Quotient?

NELSON: She's doing four A levels.

CAESAR: Ohhhhh, I seeeee…too busy being brainy to learn how to take the pill – it's all making sense, now. Aaaand let me guess Miss Chung's first name… Makeisha? Takeisha? Wakeisha?

NELSON: Just… Keisha.

CAESAR: … 'Keisha'. Is that the Swahili for 'Classy'?

LATER

KEISHA enters, with place-mats, laughing… CAESAR and DEANNA exit.

NELSON: It ain't funny, babe…

NELSON fetches a table for KEISHA to lay place-mats on…

KEISHA: What is it, then?

NELSON: It's disrespectful. And it's messed up. He's judging you and he's never even met you.

KEISHA: I'll get over it. Let's be real, my name is a bit ghetto. You should hear what my mum said about yours.

NELSON: You ain't ghetto.

KEISHA: What's wrong with ghetto?

NELSON: When ghetto looks like you… (*Kissing her.*)
'… Nuttin'…'

KEISHA: (*Kissing him back.*) '… You get me..?'

NELSON: '… Y'kna'I'msaying..?'

KEISHA: '… Innit…star..?'

More kissing… Enter CAESAR with chairs.

CAESAR: Going for twins?

NELSON: Dad!

CAESAR: Sorry, should I have knocked…?… On me own
living-room door…? (*Holding out a hand.*) Miss Keisha, I
presume?

KEISHA: Correct!

CAESAR: Thank God! I thought he'd gone out and dug up
another one already…you know what he's like…

NELSON: Dad!

DEANNA enters with cutlery.

DEANNA: Caesar. Down boy. Our guest isn't used to our
family humour – she might not know when you're joking.

CAESAR: That's easy – I'm always joking. (*Winks at KEISHA.*)
It's the laughter what keeps us from screaming, innit,
Keish?

KEISHA: I hear dat.

CAESAR: You get me?

Eyes locked, they smile. KEISHA strong, open – CAESAR wary.

DEANNA: You couldn't give us a hand bringing dinner in,
could you, Keisha?

KEISHA: Try and stop me.

KEISHA follows DEANNA off.

CAESAR: Well! Quite the little firecracker you brought home this time, son. I'm almost impressed. I thought she was gonna arm-wrestle me for moment there.

NELSON: Sha.

CAESAR: …Huh?

NELSON: Kei-sha. She ain't 'Keesh'. You make her sound like a…

CAESAR: … 'Cheesy tart'? Ahhh, look at you – It's so cute when you try and look like you could knock me out.

NELSON: She ain't a 'firecracker'. She's my…

CAESAR: … What? Your Baby-Mama-Drama to be?

NELSON: She's my… (*Looking down, quiet.*) …woman.

CAESAR: Your woman? Bwoy, Y'ave woman now? Like you is a man?

NELSON: Dad.

Offstage we hear DEANNA and KEISHA, laughing.

CAESAR: You t'ink because you too lazy, stupid or drunk to wear a Johnny that can mek you a man? It'll take more than standing about in your parent's house giving Daddy 'Evils' to make you grow balls, 'blood'. 'You get me?' '… Y'kna'I'msaying..?' 'Star'?

DEANNA enters with food, to find CAESAR and NELSON eyeballing.

DEANNA: Go and help Keisha with the plates, will ya, Nels, babe?

NELSON: It's four plates, mum, she's pregnant, not incapable.

Offstage we hear the crash of plates. CAESAR smiles. NELSON keeps staring at him for a moment, then leaves…

DEANNA: You behaving yourself?

CAESAR: Just a heartwarming little father-son Kodak moment.

DEANNA: Please Caesar.

CAESAR: Yes, dear?

DEANNA: Please…don't.

CAESAR: 'Please don't'…? Full sentences please.

DEANNA: Don't make things worse.

CAESAR: Worse? It could be worse? I'm intrigued.

DEANNA: Nelson's like you – he needs respect.

CAESAR: Ah, respect, remember that?

DEANNA: But where he's different is, he's quiet. If you push him, he'll go. Please let's just eat and be civil and listen to what they have to say. I made your favourite.

CAESAR: Shame I can't swallow nothing.

DEANNA: Swallow this. For me.

CAESAR: Am I allowed to ask questions?

DEANNA: What kind of questions?

CAESAR: The questions a father asks when his son brings a woman home.

DEANNA: What kind of questions, Caesar?

CAESAR: I don't know!! No plan – Just busking – can't a man ask questions in his own home?

KEISHA strides in with plates, NELSON follows with glasses.

KEISHA: Questions? Excellent! Any for me?

CAESAR: Funny you should say that…

They all sit.

DEANNA: Caesar, we've got years to get to know each other.

KEISHA: It's fine, Dee, I love attention. Ask me anything.

CAESAR: How do you plan to keep my son in the style to which he has regretfully become accustomed?

KEISHA: (*Smiles.*) Well, I'm not doing any ironing.

CAESAR and DEANNA exchange a look.

Actually I'm interested in management.

CAESAR: Bank management? That's solid. Let's hope they've got a crêche.

KEISHA: I mean Artist management.

CAESAR: As in Picasso?

KEISHA: As in Nelson.

CAESAR: I'm confused. Any Nelson I know?

KEISHA: Well, you've heard him rhyme, yeah?

CAESAR: I've heard him grime, is that similar?

KEISHA: You know he's had over twenty-two thousand downloads on his demo?

CAESAR: Twenty-two thousand?

KEISHA: Well, you've heard it…

DEANNA: …amazing…

KEISHA: …amazing.

CAESAR: Indeed.

KEISHA: So, we think that after we've completed sixth form college, we might apply for a loan and go for it.

CAESAR: 'Loan'?

KEISHA: I've had a building society since I was, like, born and I've got a good banking record.

DEANNA: Instead of wedding presents you could ask for cash contributions.

CAESAR: 'Wedding'?

DEANNA: Or investments.

CAESAR: 'Investments'?

DEANNA: You'll need some baby clothes… Baby shower!

CAESAR: 'Baby'?

DEANNA: We can throw it here!

CAESAR slams his fist onto the table. Everything jumps. Silence.

CAESAR: 'Baby'?

DEANNA: Are you having a senior moment, babes? This is our son, Nelson, this is his girl, Keisha, and they're having a baby. They're going to be parents. We're going to be grandparents.

CAESAR: These two? Parents? In what parallel universe? (*To KEISHA.*) You don't actually think you're having this? You don't actually believe I'm going to allow you to bring another spoilt stupid deluded ungrateful brat into existence to sponge off me, do you? You're not so high on whatever cheap trendy drug you've been snuffling behind the school bike sheds that you think I'm gonna stand by and let a seventeen-year investment go up in smoke because he's got balls for brains and you're carrying them in your pocket? Do you?

KEISHA raises a finger.

Yes?

KEISHA: This is my first time playing this game – can anyone ask a question besides you?

CAESAR: No. We've done questions. We're onto statements. No-one's having a baby, no-one's getting bank loans, no-one's becoming a popstar and NO-ONE's GETTING MARRIED! Daddy says so! You may now speak while I'm busy having this palpitation – We're still on statements.

44

KEISHA: We're not getting married.

CAESAR: Am I hallucinating? Am I in cardiac arrest and delirious? Has someone actually finally realised that I am always right?

NELSON: We're not on questions. We're on statements. We're not getting married. We're already married.

NELSON stands up.

And we're leaving.

NELSON holds out his hand, KEISHA takes it. She gets up, NELSON and KEISHA kiss DEANNA and leave… DEANNA and CAESAR sit in silence.

CAESAR: I think that went quite well, don't you?

Silence.

What? What? Oh, so I'm the bad guy? Am I the one who went out and knocked up some ball-busting bint and expected no-one to mind?

DEANNA: Actually…

CAESAR: Alright, yeah, so what? At least I didn't marry her and ruin my life! What? Don't look at me like that! You know what I mean! Why is this all on me, somehow? At least I didn't collude with our kid and keep secrets from you. You knew, didn't you? You were probably Chief Witness and Maid of bloody Honour.

DEANNA: I didn't know.

CAESAR: Then why aren't you as freaked out as I am? That's your little boy! You're supposed to hate any woman who takes him away from you! Why are you so fucking reasonable?

DEANNA: 'Cause that's my little boy and I don't want to lose him.

CAESAR: You think I do? He's my boy too, you know.

DEANNA: You told his wife to have an abortion.

CAESAR: She's seventeen! They're seventeen!

DEANNA: We were seventeen!

CAESAR: Wake up woman! Their seventeen ain't like our seventeen! These kids think poverty is only five pound credit on their mobile and no Sky Movies Plus! You think they're ready to get up of morning before it's light and go out and sweat bullets for a living, working two, three jobs each? You heard her – She ain't doing no ironing! He's gonna be a grimy Pop Idol and she's gonna be his manager financing his inevitable rise to fame and fortune off her Post Office savings book! They ain't got a bleedin' clue! They don't know they're born! They ain't working class like us – They're entitled middle-class me-generation Blair-Babies and if you took away their microwaves they would starve to fucking death! You sweated for a living! You sacrificed and you done without and you suffered. I know – I suffered with you. You broke your back raising a brown baby in a racist world – You've been called a nigger-lover to your face. You heard grown men and women teaching their kids to sing, 'White but not Quite' to your baby in its pram. You've seen him searched on the street just for being there and being black. You've seen schools fail him and pop videos misguide him and peers try to drag him down the wrong road. You've seen how harsh life can be. And now – knowing all that you know – knowing all the tribulations them two kids have got in store, you're still determined to indulge their doomed little delusions as if they were actual plans – when they ain't plans – they're blue-prints for crucifixion. And yet you have the audacity to make me the villain – when it's you what's being cruel. I know you believe it's all good intentions – but the real truth is that you can't handle the truth – you don't want to deal with the reality that our son has thrown away his youth and fucked up his life, just like we did. You don't want to face the fact that we – that's both you and me by the way – have failed and our son is a statistic.

DEANNA: I have not failed and I ain't a fuck-up. And neither's my son. Reality? What world are you living in? Who in this world has a life that goes to a plan? Parenting is messy. Life is messy. Yes, we never had a plan no money and no clue – and here we are sat in our dream house, because we had each other.

CAESAR: And who's our son got? Do you know her family? Her background? Do you really believe that pampered little madam is as strong as you had to be?

DEANNA: … I don't know.

CAESAR: You don't know!

DEANNA: I know one thing though. I know our son. And if he says he's having a baby, we both know – we can shout all we want, but the reality is: it's time to start buying nappies. The reality is: there's a grandchild coming. And whether this marriage works or not, it's our job to see him through it. And if they've got trials to face, we shouldn't be one of them. 'Cause the fact is that they are not us – they've got some savings and however pathetic an amount it is – it's more than we had – Yeah, they're reckless, idealistic, unrealistic teenage plans – but they're making plans. Not whining about sacrifice and ruined lives. Not crying about being fuck-ups – Because they don't see their baby as the death of their old dream – they see it as the birth of their new one. They're approaching their future together with determination and commitment – We never even got married. No, Caesar – they ain't got a clue. But they have got me and they have got you and they need our support – because our son's got the one thing we wanted for him above everything – hope. He's got hope, Caesar and that's a rare and beautiful thing – And that's the reality – and you have to deal with it.

CAESAR: I am dealing with it.

DEANNA: How? Our son steps up to his responsibility and responds to this crisis with honour. He don't run, he don't demand a DNA test on some talk show – he does what once upon a time used to be called 'The Right thing', brings his bride home and you insult her.

CAESAR: I only called her Keesh for God's sake! I was trying to be affectionate.

DEANNA: 'Sket'? 'Bint'?

CAESAR: It weren't personal! Ain't no-one got a sense of humour no more?

DEANNA: You insulted our daughter-in-law, Caesar.

CAESAR: What law? They're underage! 'Insulted her'… You mean I embarrassed you.

DEANNA: (*Shakes her head.*) You humiliated me. You embarrassed yourself. And you shamed the family.

DEANNA gets up, wearily and starts to clear the table.

CAESAR: What are we, the Mafia? 'Shamed the family?' Such a Drama Mama! Where you going with my dinner? I'm hungry.

DEANNA leaves his plate in front of him.

Wasting good food. That I paid for… You mus' be mad… So, you're not talking to me now? You're choosing him over me?

DEANNA: Is that what you want me to do? Choose?

CAESAR: No. But if I did, who would you choose?

DEANNA: You want me to choose.

CAESAR: No. But who would you choose? See, that's where we're different. You would choose him over me every time.

DEANNA: No, where we're different is I could never choose.

Pause

48

CAESAR: But if you had to choose? Between being a mother and being a lover?

DEANNA: I'd choose family.

Long pause.

CAESAR: I'm not coping with this very well, am I?

DEANNA: It ain't your best work, babes.

CAESAR: And now you despise me?

DEANNA: Don't be silly.

CAESAR: Or am I beneath your contempt? What can I do to sort this out?

DEANNA: You can fetch our baby back home.

CAESAR: He ain't our baby no more, babes, ain't you heard? He's a married man.

DEANNA: He's our baby. Fetch him back. Today.

EVITA'S LOUNGE

EVITA enters with a sofa. DEANNA leaves with the table.

CAESAR: How the hell did he get married at seventeen, anyway? I'm getting it annulled.

EVITA: And he'll realise you have his best interests at heart and love you more than ever.

CAESAR: He don't have to love me. I'm his dad, not his homie.

EVITA: 'Homie'?

CAESAR: It's my job to be hated.

EVITA: Congratulations on a job well done.

CAESAR gives EVITA a look.

I'm your baby sister, it's my job to be annoying.

By now DEANNA has gone and CAESAR and EVITA are sharing her sofa.

CAESAR: How can my son be having a baby? He hasn't finished growing yet! He's still in school.

EVITA: Ain't we all?

CAESAR: And married? Who the hell gets married these days? I ain't even married yet and my son is married?

EVITA: Always was a bit of a show-off, bless him… (*Off CAESAR's look.*)…the little bastard. Do people still say Homie?

CAESAR: How would I know? I'm a dad. He ain't been round here, yet?

EVITA: No.

Enter NELSON, who plonks down on the sofa. EVITA is now in two scenes simultaneously.

NELSON: He ain't been round here yet?

EVITA: No.

NELSON / CAESAR: Good!

CAESAR: Arrogant little twat.

NELSON: Miserable old git.

CAESAR: When he does come round don't let him in, alright? And definitely don't let him stay when he asks.

EVITA: As if I'd ever say yes to that.

NELSON: If he calls tell him you ain't heard from me, yeah? Can I cotch here tonight?

EVITA: As if I'd ever say no to you.

CAESAR: It's time he found out what being a man really takes.

NELSON: Thanks Auntie Evita, you're a star – have you got Sky Sports?

EVITA: I thought you'd be staying at Keisha's?

NELSON: Her mum's old school. She won't let mans stay over and alla dat.

EVITA: Even if they're married to her daughter?

NELSON: She don't know. If she found out she's get us annulled. She's crazy like that.

EVITA: Worse than your dad?

NELSON: No-one's worse than my dad. 'Cept Keisha's mum. So, he ain't called or nothing?

CAESAR: He ain't called or nothing?

EVITA: No.

NELSON: See, he don't care anyway.

CAESAR: Like I care, anyway.

NELSON: He's glad I'm gone.

CAESAR: No texts? (*Grabbing her phone.*) Let me check your phone. He's probably at that sket's place, eating them out of house and home. They're welcome to him.

NELSON: All he talks about is how much I eat, how much electricity I use, how much he could get for renting out my room.

CAESAR: (*Chucking down phone.*) You don't know where she lives, do you?

NELSON: I was a mistake anyway. If it weren't for me, he'd have been movie star.

EVITA: Is that what he told you?

NELSON: Only once a day, like. If he'd only had another ten years – He could have had some fun, could have pressed some girls, he could have conquered the world. But he screwed up. He had me.

EVITA: Nelson. Your Dad loves you.

NELSON: Is that what he told you?

EVITA: He don't have to tell me.

NELSON: Has he ever said he loved me?

EVITA: Of course he has.

NELSON: When?

EVITA: A million times.

NELSON: When? When has my dad ever said I love you to anyone? Has he ever said it to you? I know. He don't have to. He's Caesar.

NELSON leaves.

EVITA looks at CAESAR who sits staring into space.

EVITA: (*To CAESAR.*) Is there anything you want me to say if I see him?

CAESAR: No. (*Silence.*) … Yeah.

… No. Like what?

POOL HALL

Enter CHE playing pool, as EVITA leaves. He hands CAESAR a pool cue…

CHE: I dunno.

CAESAR: What does a man say to someone who's gone and thrown away every thing you've worked your nuts off your entire life to give them?

CHE: Er…

CAESAR: Exactly. What is there to say? What would you say?

CHE: Er, hmmm…

CAESAR: Exactly. What would your dad say if you got some slapper up the duff what was too lazy and selfish to get an abortion and then married her without even having the decency to at least elope and stay out of his face?

CHE: Ummm…

CAESAR: Exactly! He would be speechless. He wouldn't come round to your best friend looking for you, prepared to discuss the issue man to man. He would be stunned speechless by your reckless audacity. He would be gutted.

CHE: I don't know my dad.

CAESAR: You don't know your dad, man?

CHE: No, man.

CAESAR: Sorry, man. Me neither…exactly, see! He's lucky to even have a dad. Most of 'em piss off as soon as they realise a responsibility's on the way. And now we see why! I used to cuss my dad for doing one before I could talk. Now I envy him. Smart old bastard got away before I could answer back. I was a mug – I stuck it out – didn't want my son to do what I done – grow up without someone to teach him how to shave and all that. How to walk like a man. I was gonna be a role model. I didn't count on him copying all my mistakes an' all. A father before he can vote or drive? Do you ever hear from your dad?

CHE: He's dead.

CAESAR: Oh. Right. Sorry.

CHE: Why? Ain't your fault.

CAESAR: At last, something that ain't my fault. What happened, do you know?

CHE: He died in prison.

CAESAR: Wow. Stabbed, er, 'shanked'?

CHE: AIDS.

CAESAR: Wow. That's really messed up.

CHE: Worse than a shank, yeah?

CAESAR: That's not what I meant – I didn't mean that… It's all messed up. Prison. Shanks. AIDS. Death…

CHE: …dads…

CAESAR: You miss him?

CHE: Never really knew him. Do I miss the idea of him? Depends.

CAESAR: On?

CHE: On the day. Like, when I'm round yours, yeah, and we're watching the game, like, and you're shouting and laughing and a little bit tipsy and you sit with your arms round Nelson, it's like, whoa, deep, I wonder how that would be…like… But then other times…

CAESAR: What other times?

CHE: You know, the rest of the time. Well, not all the time, but you know average times when you're you know, saying things and you know…

CAESAR: No. What things?

CHE: You know.

CAESAR: What things?

CHE: Nothing.

CAESAR: What things?

CHE: Like, when you're calling him names an' that…calling him stupid and whatever…

CAESAR: When do I ever call him stupid?

CHE: (*Shrugs and laughs.*) When don't you?

CAESAR: I'm just having a laugh.

CHE: Oh. Okay.

CAESAR: It's just banter, Che. It's just me steering him back to the right path in a light-hearted manner. It's what dads do.

CHE: ... Exactly.

CAESAR: What the bloodclaat is that meant to mean?

CHE: (*Quickly.*) Nothing.

CAESAR: Are you judging me?

CHE: (*Quickly.*) No.

CAESAR: And now you're acting all scared so I'll feel like a monster – I ain't big-foot, I'm a dad! Alright, sometimes I get loud – so?! I used to wish I had a big loud bloke who'd stick around and shout at me and give a shit about the things I was doing to screw up my life. And here I am and I'm Sasquatch. Wishing I had a dad I could go to and ask – what now? What do I do? How do I save my son from himself?

Enter PRECIOUS RAMSAY – she is cooking. CHE leaves.

PRECIOUS: Licks.

CAESAR: Actually mother, right now what I'm looking for is a way to get through to my son.

PRECIOUS: Licks.

CAESAR: And before that I just need to get him to come home.

PRECIOUS: Licks.

CAESAR: Which means that I'll have to start by tracking him down.

PRECIOUS: Licks.

CAESAR: I'm supposed to use 'licks' to find my kid?

PRECIOUS: Go to his friend, give him licks till he tells you where your son is, then find your son and give him licks till he runs home to his mum, then the two of you give him licks till he's too damn scared to run away. Licks is the Father the Son and the Holy Ghost. Licks is like Vaseline – it works for everything. It worked for you. It worked for me. Licks.

CAESAR: Is that what you think?

PRECIOUS: It's what I know. See how you never went to prison, like every other loser kid off our estate? That's 'cause you were raised with moral backbone. That's 'cause you were raised with discipline.

CAESAR: Mother, I got a girl pregnant at seventeen, you got knocked up at sixteen and a half!

PRECIOUS: And if wasn't for licks I'd've got pregnant at ten!

Enter EVITA, back from the shop with a cooking ingredient.

EVITA: You're exaggerating, mother..!

PRECIOUS: I ain't gonna lie – I was a proper little skank! The only thing that stopped me running away to be a stripper at twelve was the terror of getting found, getting caught and getting licks. I knew who ran tings!

CAESAR: I think my son knows who run 'tings', thank you, mother.

PRECIOUS: You think all that barking means any thing to him? All he hears is blah blah blah woof woof woof! Your grandmother was right – What you can't hear…

EVITA / PRECIOUS: …you must feel…

EVITA: … This the 21st century mother – ain't you read the papers? Licks have been discredited.

PRECIOUS: And what's happened? The world has turned to shit!

EVITA: Mother! Language!

PRECIOUS: I am over fifty, the point of living this long is to use whatever words I want and I say the world has turned to shit! Why? Because the pickney them confuse! They're craving a moral compass! All over this country, kids are running the streets at all hours of the night, like stray dog, rifling through the bin bags of humanity – scavenging in skips overflowing with discarded decency, morality and plain old-fashioned good manners. Kids are hungry for guidance and for a firm hand. Like you were and your parents before you. Hungry. That's why I raised my hand to you – I was feeding you. And whether you know it or not, you were grateful.

EVITA: Thanks for telling us.

PRECIOUS: Find your boy drag him backside home and give him the gift of licks. He will thank you for it.

CAESAR: Did I ever thank you?

PRECIOUS: You will. You're still young.

CAESAR: We hated you.

EVITA: Why you dragging me into it?

CAESAR: Okay, I hated you. I hated you, mother. Every time you raised your hand. Made me fetch the belt… I hated you.

PRECIOUS: If you've never been hated, you've never been a parent. That's the system. I hated your grandmother. And now I worship that woman for the Goddess she is. You hated me and now you're standing in my kitchen pleading for advice to help you with your delinquent child.

EVITA: … Who hates him. (*Apologetic face.*) …sorry bruv.

CAESAR: He said that he hates me?

PRECIOUS: Welcome to the system, son.

EVITA: He don't really hate you.

CAESAR: But he said that? He hates me?

EVITA: He said you hate him. He's just young and he's upset cause you called his girl a sket and a cheesy tart.

PRECIOUS: You said that? Boy, you need to wash out your mouth! What's a sket?

EVITA: A skank.

PRECIOUS: Oh.

EVITA: As in when you were ten you were a proper little sket.

PRECIOUS: Oh. Pass the salt.

CAESAR: You really hated Nana Grace?

PRECIOUS: I tried to hire a hit man on her.

CAESAR: Nana Grace never gave you licks.

PRECIOUS: I'm still putting cocoa butter on the scars. Nana Grace never gave you licks. Just like I never gave Nelson licks.

CAESAR: I just thought you liked him better than me.

PRECIOUS: Why you have to talk stupid?

CAESAR: What are you doing?

PRECIOUS: What's it look like I'm doing – don't start.

EVITA: Mother's cooking.

CAESAR: Cooking?!

PRECIOUS: Why you gotta say it like that?

CAESAR: Cooking? You burn salad! Cooking?

EVITA: (*Handing him a cookbook.*) From a recipe.

CAESAR: A recipe?

EVITA: I've already alerted the fire brigade.

CAESAR: Mother, what the hell is going on?

PRECIOUS: If I'm gonna be a great-grandmother, I should be able to cook.

CAESAR: You were a mother who couldn't cook –

EVITA: – And a grandmother who couldn't cook –

CAESAR: Why change the habits of a lifetime?

PRECIOUS: You focus on your lifetime, I'll focus on mine. I know I wasn't the perfect mum. I know I was too young. I know I was too wild. But when it came down to the wire, I never lost my kids, not to the social, not to peer pressure, not to a life of crime, and not to themselves. I know it shouldn't be an achievement that your kids stayed out of jail and never become crack-heads, but the sad fact remains – round here it is. And I achieved it…with licks. Pass the plantain.

Enter DEANNA with a bed. PRECIOUS and EVITA leave. DEANNA and CAESAR kick off their shoes and curl up watching TV.

DEANNA: You actually told her that you'd hated her?

CAESAR: And she says: 'Pass the plantain'.

DEANNA: Wow. Are you alright?

CAESAR: I'm jealous. So much confidence in her authority. I say, 'I hated you' – she says, 'you were meant to – pass the plantain' …and…? I hand it to her. End of discussion. She's right – I'm over it. She's always been in control and she's never – not for a second – lost it. She's text-book parenting.

DEANNA: There's more to being a parent than control.

CAESAR: (*sighs.*) So much more. And I can't even manage the basics. I can't even get respect in my own home.

DEANNA: Bullying don't get you respected, babes. It don't even get you obeyed. Just lied to. (*She touches him, gently.*) You're not over it. You've never been over it. You told me – You remember every beating – Every strike – you told me.

CAESAR pulls away from her.

Caesar…

CAESAR: That's my mother you're talking about…

DEANNA: You what?

CAESAR: … That you're calling a bully – my mother.

DEANNA: I never called her a…

CAESAR: My *mother*, alright?

Pause.

DEANNA: Sorry.

Pause.

CAESAR: Occasionally sometimes she might have gone a bit far. A woman on her own. No man to deliver the discipline. Sometimes they can overcompensate. But without respect for the parent a child is lost. Family becomes anarchy.

DEANNA: See, that's where we're lucky. We're not alone. We're a team. And we've done well. Nelson's always been a good boy.

CAESAR: … Not any more.

DEANNA: Always been quiet…

CAESAR: … Not any more…

DEANNA: …always done exactly what he's been told…

CAESAR: … Until now.

DEANNA: And you never raised a hand to him. You never even raised your voice. Not really. Not in real anger… Until now. And what's happened? He's rebelled. Just like you done. You're conveniently forgetting – but you did. The harder you were pushed, the faster you ran… Right to me.

CAESAR: …see? It weren't all bad…

They kiss.

DEANNA: You flatter me, sir…

CAESAR: You know what? Sod the kid…we can always make another one…

DEANNA: Now *that's* a plan!

CAESAR: … Ow, baby!! Come to Daddy!!

DEANNA: (*Laughing.*) Shhh! Caesar!!

CAESAR: No kid plus empty nest equals Mo' noise! Quick, before the brat comes crawling back home! Let's get loud, babygirl!

DEANNA: He's home.

CAESAR: He's…?

DEANNA: He's been in his room all evening. Packing.

CAESAR shoves her away and gets up…

Caesar – breathe!

CAESAR: Packing? (*Pulling on his shoes.*) I thought you wanted him to come home?

DEANNA: I did! He did! And we had a little chat. Don't you think it would good for him to have a break from us?

CAESAR: Don't you think it would've been good to consult me? Team-mate?

CAESAR heads off…

DEANNA: Caesar!

NELSON'S BEDROOM

CAESAR finds NELSON packing.

CAESAR: Ooops sorry. Did I forget to knock again? Planning a little vacation? Checking out of the flea-pit Ramsay Hotel and going five-star, is that it? Oh! I see! We're moving out! We're independent now! Don't need stupid dad to pay the stupid bills and break his stupid back keeping a roof over our smart smug little head. 'I'm a man! I'm the daddy!'

DEANNA: Caesar!

CAESAR: 'I'M THE FUCKING DADDY!'

NELSON turns to go.

Excuse, me, but where do you think you're going with that suitcase? You don't want that suitcase – Daddy's money paid for that suitcase. That's tainted, that suitcase. You don't want that. You're gonna put it down.

CAESAR takes the suitcase – bangs it down.

You're gonna put that fucking suitcase down and you're gonna empty it!

CAESAR rips open the suitcase…

Empty it! EMPTY IT!

…starts pulling clothes out and scattering them.

You don't need these stupid fucking clothes – that Daddy paid for – you don't need these! Fuck 'em! Fuck all of 'em! You're walking out with your head held high. Proud independent man. Proud! You can pay your own way! Buy your own shit!!!

KEISHA: (*Offstage.*) Nelson?

CAESAR: Oh, here she is – trouble and strife. Ball and chain. Her indoors... In here, Missus!

KEISHA enters.

She sees clothes strewn everywhere. CAESAR standing there, panting. DEANNA watching. And NELSON still and silent.

KEISHA: You alright?

CAESAR: Nelson's not speaking, love. He's maintaining a dignified silence. He's above all this, ain't you big man? It just ain't worth, it, innit?

DEANNA: You two should go.

CAESAR: Yeah. You two should go.

KEISHA reaches out and carefully takes NELSON's hand.

KEISHA: Let's go babe.

NELSON starts to let himself be led away.

CAESAR: But not with them shoes.

KEISHA and NELSON stop.

Not with them shoes that fascist Daddy paid for with his filthy money. You don't want nothing of his. This is a clean break – can't make a clean break in Daddy's shoes.

Pause. Then NELSON steps out of his shoes.

Thank you. And the hoodie please. Don't want Daddy's hoodie.

NELSON takes his hoodie off.

Trousers.

NELSON undoes his belt and takes his trousers off. He stands there in his underwear and socks.

Clean break...

NELSON pulls off his socks, and is about to pull off his pants when…

DEANNA: Okay, that's enough.

DEANNA steps forward and stops NELSON. She picks up the clothes, trying to hand them to NELSON, who does not take them.

You've both made your points – Nelson, just go okay? We'll talk when everyone's a bit more calmed down, yeah?

CAESAR: Yeah, kids, scamper off to your love nest, before the spotlight turns on Mummy and she's revealed for what she is really.

DEANNA: What am I really?

CAESAR: Before everyone susses how all this conflict was caused by Mummy Dearest.

DEANNA: By me?

CAESAR: Yeah, you! You you you! Always gotta be perfect, ain't you? Perfect mother, perfect lover, perfect wife! You've used up all the perfect! And what's left for the rest of us?… Imperfect! You've spoilt us! Hippy-dippy best friend earth mother! Washing everything, cooking everything, understanding everything, being right about everything, loving us no matter what we say and what we do, we're spoilt rotten! We're out of control!

DEANNA: Caesar, babes, what are you on about? You ain't making no sense.

CAESAR: I stopped making sense the day I clapped eyes on you. Before you, it was all mapped out, meet some slapper, get her knocked up, oops oh, well, change postcodes – collide with three more babymothers scattered round the capital, spend me life dodging payments, then find the right woman at thirty-nine, see the error of me ways and finally start contemplating maturity. Instead I meet you at the tender age of stupid seventeen and you only make me go and fall in love, doncha? You only make me do the right thing and practically marry you! And then you have to go and get yourself pregnant with the most beautiful well-behaved baby on the planet and you hold down a job and hold our family together while I follow my dream and set up a business – and you make it all so plain-sailing painlessly fucking easy, you fucking witch! You even made it fun! You set me up! I was so blissed-out I never saw it coming, did I?

DEANNA: Saw what coming?

CAESAR: Puberty! The little bastard's balls drop and he's like a bleedin' gremlin splashed with water! Cccccrrrraaaahhhhhh! Evil, arrogant little demon! Our cute cuddly offspring's gone from Nelson Jekyll to Napoleon Hyde, cock of the walk, (*Demonstrating a pimp roll.*) Dragging his foot suh, like him a man now! And if I dare to raise my voice about it, I'm a bully. What am I supposed to do when he comes in at one-thirty on a school-night towing a babe with a bun in the oven? Take away his TV, his iPod, his mobile and his laptop and his MTV Base and lock him in his room every evening till he's thirty? What am I supposed to do?

KEISHA raises a finger.

Sorry, Teesha, Extrecia, Alopecia, darling – but I think you'll find that this is a family conversation.

DEANNA: Oh, Caesar…

NELSON: She's my wife.

CAESAR: Not in the eyes of the law.

NELSON: She's my wife. Her name is Keisha Ramsay. And she's my wife. (*Indicating DEANNA.*) And that woman is my mother and your wife. We are a family. Not your audience, not your punch-bags. Not your bitches. A family.

CAESAR: My family. And this is my house. And you can stand here in my house and hate me all you want – But I will have respect.

NELSON: I don't hate you.

NELSON walks up to his father and looks him the face.

I pity you.

CAESAR head-butts NELSON.

DEANNA: Caesar! }{ KEISHA: Shit!

NELSON drops to his knees. His nose is bleeding.

DEANNA: Oh my God, what }{ KEISHA: Shit! Nelson! Are
are you... you al...

CAESAR: Nobody move.

DEANNA and KEISHA stop in their tracks.

My house. My family. My rules. (*To NELSON.*) Fetch my belt.

NELSON looks up at CAESAR.

It's in my jeans. There. Beside you. On my floor.

NELSON sees the jeans he has just taken off. Shaking. He picks them up. Pulls out the belt. Hands it to CAESAR.

(*Looping the end of the belt round his hand.*) You feel sorry for me now?

NELSON looks him in the eye.

NELSON: More than ever.

CAESAR stares back. Then with a roar, shoves NELSON over and starts to whip his behind. KEISHA cries out and starts to weep hiding her eyes in DEANNA's arms. CAESAR grunts with each blow, NELSON does not cry. DEANNA can stand it no more – she cries out!

DEANNA: Caesar!

CAESAR stops. He drops the belt to the floor. He walks off. The sound of KEISHA's crying and NELSON and DEANNA's breathing.

INTERVAL.

SEVENTEEN YEARS AGO – FOOTBALL FIELD

CAESAR: You what?

DEANNA: (*Smiling nervously.*) You heard.

CAESAR: You're what?

DEANNA: Please don't make me say it again…

CAESAR: You sure?

DEANNA: I've triple-checked, trust me.

CAESAR: And you're telling me now?

DEANNA: I've come straight here from finding out!

CAESAR: I'm in the middle of a match!

DEANNA: So?

CAESAR: It's the semi-final!

DEANNA: 'Semi-final'?

CAESAR: You couldn't wait half-an-hour?

DEANNA: 'Semi-bleedin' final'? We're having a baby!

CAESAR: We're two-nil up!

DEANNA: WE'RE HAVING! A BLEEDIN' BABY!!!

They look around at everyone looking at them – he grins nervously. DEANNA looks at CAESAR.

At least I am. About, like, twenty-years earlier than scheduled. I only enrolled in sixth-form college on Wednesday, I'm supposed to get five As, go up to Cambridge, do an exchange year at Yale, become an intern at a major corporation, get mentored by a skinny white woman in a black dress and end up living in a Co-op in Manhattan. You think I've got time to fall for a scrub and end up in a council flat with a brood of borstal boy brats. You think I want to stand here on a windy muddy Sunday morning with you blaming me for trapping you while I pray that you love me and will stand by me or at least will believe that you're the only one and this is your kid? You think I'm prepared to give it all up and face my mum, dad and brothers and gamble my every future dream and hopes on the fact that I am stupidly, pathetically, helplessly in love with you?

Pause.

I dunno…I hope so.

They melt into one another's arms..

DEANNA: I'm sorry babes…

CAESAR: No, I'm sorry, babes…

DEANNA: No, I'm sorry…

CAESAR: No, I'm sorry – You're pregnant. (*Smiling, nuzzling her.*) We're pregnant… No wonder I'm feeling sick…

They giggle, nose to nose.

… Am I showing yet? I do love you, you know. Thank God, seeing as I'm stuck with you.

DEANNA: Are you?

CAESAR: You know it, gyal… All the way – End of the line…

A football hits CAESAR on the back of the head.

Oy! Watch it man! We're pregnant!

TODAY: THE RAMSAY HOME

DEANNA, picking up NELSON's scattered clothes – folding each one and putting it back into the discarded suitcase. CAESAR watching her. He picks up something.

DEANNA: Leave it.

CAESAR: (*Starts to fold it.*) It's cool…

DEANNA: Leave it.

She holds out a hand, he gives her the item. She takes it and starts to fold it.

Just leave it.

CAESAR watches her.

CAESAR: Jesus Christ, woman, it weren't nothing but a couple of licks. He knows…he knows he pushed me too far. He knows he left me no choice. He's just sulking, he'll be back. My mother used to make us fetch the curtain rod and she used to whip us with that. She took a Scalextrix track to me once. Chucked the house phone at me… I laugh about it now.

DEANNA picks up the belt. She looks at it.

He'll laugh about it one day. Any money.

DEANNA puts the belt down on the ground, picks up her own coat. She puts it on.

Where you going? You going somewhere? Where you going? You coming back? When?… Ever?… Never? So that's it? You just don't love me no more? Come on, say it.

DEANNA starts to leave – CAESAR steps in front of her.

Say it! You don't love me. Say it.

DEANNA: You know I can't say it.

CAESAR: Then how can you leave?

DEANNA: How can I stay?

SEVENTEEN YEARS AGO – COUNCIL ESTATE LANDING

DEANNA taking down washing off a line. CAESAR is following her with a basket, she puts the clothes in it.

CAESAR: Victor.

DEANNA: Victor.

CAESAR: What's wrong with Victor?

DEANNA: Nothing. It's a bit old school.

CAESAR: I thought we liked old school.

DEANNA: We do. I dunno, Victor. 'Vic'. hmm. 'Victor'.

CAESAR: Means winner.

DEANNA: And if it's girl, Victoria?

CAESAR: It ain't a girl.

DEANNA: How do you know?

CAESAR: I felt him kick. It ain't a girl.

DEANNA: Girls can kick.

CAESAR: Not like this. It's a boy. I know it.

DEANNA: Do you want a boy?

CAESAR: Dunno. I should do. Girls break dad's hearts. But boys break mum's. I don't want no-one breaking your heart. (*Kisses her.*) 'Cept me. (*Kisses her again.*) Not even me.

DEANNA smiles, goes back to the washing.

DEANNA: So you want a name that means winner?

CAESAR: Names are important. Every time someone calls you, it sends a message – Like mine. Every time someone calls me Caesar, I'm reminded of the kind of man I was born to be.

DEANNA: So what kind of man do we want our son to be?

CAESAR: Proud.

DEANNA: Principled.

CAESAR: Powerful.

DEANNA: Persistent.

CAESAR: Prime Minister.

DEANNA: President.

CAESAR: ... Nelson.

DEANNA: Nelson? As in Trafalgar?

CAESAR: As in Mandela. Strength. Courage. Wisdom. Dignity. Humanity. Nelson.

DEANNA: And if he's a girl? Nelsa?

CAESAR: He ain't a girl. (*He kisses her.*) He's Mummy's other little heartbreaker.

They kiss, as the scene changes round to them back to...

TODAY – THE RAMSAY HOME

DEANNA and CAESAR looking at one another, she is holding the suitcase.

She walks past CAESAR, their bodies brushing, his body gently blown aside like a leaf, his heart cracking... and she is gone.

CAESAR: Go then. All of you.

He picks up the belt.

Go.

He puts it through the loops of his own trousers.

Fuck all of you.

He pulls out a console and slumps back into his sofa, snapping on a video game and starts to play.

Fuck! All! Of you! My house! My rules! My way!

He spreads himself across the sofa, hogging it.

My house! Finally! Mine all mine!

He pulls out the TV remote.

Watch what I want…

He snaps on the TV.

FX: Roar of a goal being scored.

Yeeeeaaaaaahhhhhhhh!

He snaps on the dvd

FX: Soundtrack of 300…

CAESAR / 300: 'This! Is! Sparta!!!!'

CAESAR leaps up with the remote, snapping on the stereo and dancing over the sofa. He finds a beer and guzzles it, letting the foam run down his t-shirt and over the sofa.

CAESAR: Oops!

He screws up the can and defiantly drops it on the ground.

CAESAR snaps the TV to a porn channel and settles down to watch…

FX: Gasping, girly lesbian sex…

CAESAR watches eagerly at first, start to slump, rallies himself, forcing interest, but can't sustain it. As he pulls another beer out of the sofa and downs that, his eyes glaze into maudlin depression until the TV picture turns to snow and hiss and he is staring into space.

Enter EVITA.

EVITA: Bloody Hell!

She takes the remote from CAESAR's limp fingers and snaps off the TV.

Having fun are we?

CAESAR: House to ourself – eating and drinking what we like when we like with no interruption. We're having the time of our life.

EVITA: I'm glad someone is. You stink by the way.

CAESAR: And you need to find a bra what fits properly – no-one's perfect. (*Finding a biscuit in the sofa and eating it.*) What's that mean, 'Glad someone is?'

EVITA: You what?

CAESAR: You heard. What's wrong?

EVITA: What's wrong with what?

CAESAR: What's wrong with you?

EVITA: Why should something be wrong with me?

CAESAR: Something's always wrong with you.

EVITA: I don't wanna talk about it.

CAESAR: Since when do you not wanna talk about anything?

EVITA: You'll only kick off.

CAESAR: Why will I kick off?

EVITA: You're already kicking off.

CAESAR: If I wanna kick off, I'll kick off, alright?…Why am I kicking off?… Is it a man?

EVITA: Well…

CAESAR: (*Instantly aggressive.*) It's a man? You been seeing a man? What man?

EVITA: See how you stay?

CAESAR: What man?

EVITA: I'm nearly thirty, Caesar. I ain't a virgin, alright?

CAESAR: (*Jumping up as if burned.*) Gyal! Why you gotta say them things to me?

EVITA: You're psychotic.

CAESAR: What's he done to you?

EVITA: Nothing.

CAESAR: What the fuck's he done?

EVITA: I can handle it.

CAESAR: You don't have to handle it – I'll handle it – if he's messing you about, I'll handle it.

EVITA: I don't want you handling it – and I don't want you going round there.

CAESAR: Round where?

EVITA: Nowhere!

CAESAR: ROUND WHERE?

EVITA: My place.

CAESAR: YOUR PLACE?

EVITA: He's round my place.

CAESAR: What's he doing round your place? It's ten o'clock at night!

EVITA: Don't worry, he's leaving.

CAESAR: Good.

EVITA: He's leaving me.

CAESAR: He's dumping you?

EVITA: Thanks for the tact, bruv.

CAESAR: He's dumping my sister? Is he mad?

EVITA: I didn't say he was dumping, I said he was leaving.

CAESAR: Man's been living there? Since when?

EVITA: Since you been locked in the house eating take-away and rotting from the groin outwards, that's when. While you've been having the time of your life, some of us have just been having lives, mate.

CAESAR: Do you…love this loser?

EVITA: Yeah. (*Sighs.*) And he's leaving.

CAESAR: Sod him. If he don't want you, he's a nutter, you're well shot. What's this one done? Did he cheat on you? I'll knock the fucker's teeth out.

EVITA: Sweet of you, but I don't think my motherly instincts will be best served by my dear heart getting his teeth knocked out.

CAESAR: Motherly?

EVITA: I know! Innit? Me! I totally never saw it coming neither. There's me wandering round my life, drinking, staying out late and blissfully reckless and heedless, when he moves in and suddenly I'm jumping out of my skin at the deafening chiming of the biological clock.

CAESAR: Evita, sis, trust me, you don't want kids, they'll rip your guts out and use 'em for skipping rope.

EVITA: You're right.

CAESAR: You're better off alone.

EVITA: (*Looking round.*) So I see.

CAESAR looks round at the pigsty. EVITA sniffs back a tear.

CAESAR: (*Jumping up.*) Bastard! You stay here, yeah?

EVITA: Caesar – I can handle it!

CAESAR: *I'm* handling it!

EVITA: I'm coming with you!

CAESAR: No!

24 YEARS AGO

CAESAR is nearly eleven, EVITA is seven.

EVITA: I'm coming!

CAESAR: Piss off!

EVITA: I'm telling mum!

CAESAR: Tell her!

EVITA: I will! I'll tell her you went out and left me on my own.

CAESAR: So? She left you on your own.

EVITA: No, she left me with you!

CAESAR: I'm only ten!

EVITA: I'm only seven!

CAESAR: I'm supposed to be irresponsible!

EVITA: And I'm supposed to be a tell-tale! She'll give you licks!

CAESAR: It's only for a minute!

EVITA: No it ain't! You're leaving me and going out to play!

CAESAR: Don't talk stupid, It's gone ten o'clock, fool!

EVITA: Where you going then?

CAESAR: None of your business!

EVITA: Where you going?   } { CAESAR: None ya business
Where you going?   None ya business
Where you going?   None ya business
                                      I'm going to my dad's!

EVITA stares.

CAESAR: Alright? Satisfied?

EVITA: Your Dad's?

CAESAR: You heard.

EVITA: You got a dad?

CAESAR: Everyone's got a dad, fool!

EVITA: No-one in my class has got one.

CAESAR: Course they have, they just don't realise.

EVITA: So I've got one?

CAESAR: Even you.

EVITA: Why can't I go with you to your dad's?

CAESAR: 'Cause.

EVITA: 'Cause what?

CAESAR: 'Cause.

EVITA: 'Cause what?

CAESAR: 'Cause I'm only going for five minutes.

EVITA: You said one minute!

CAESAR: I just wanna look in the window – that's all. Five minutes – then I'll come back. I'm going on my bike.

EVITA: How'd you know where he is?

CAESAR: He called up.

EVITA: On the phone?

CAESAR: He talked to me. Last week. He called up and he talked to me – Said he was coming over on Saturday to take me to bowling. But he never. Anyway, I found out his address. And I'm just gonna go and look. And you can't come.

EVITA: How'd you find it?

CAESAR: I'm clever.

EVITA: Can you find out where my dad lives?

CAESAR: No.

EVITA: Why not?

CAESAR: 'Cause I can't… I'm sorry.

I'll only be ten minutes. I just want to look, then I'll come back, and I'll read you a story.

EVITA: What if mum comes back?

CAESAR: She won't. I'll bring you back something from the corner shop, alright?

He leads her to the sofa.

You sit here and you watch telly, yeah? (*Handing her the remote.*) You can watch what you want…and you won't even miss me.

CAESAR starts to go.

EVITA: Yeah I will. (*Jumping up.*) I'm coming with you!

CAESAR: (*Running.*) Noooooooooooooo!

EVITA: (*Chasing.*) I'm comiiiiiiiiiiiing!

A window comes on – CAESAR and EVITA end up behind it, peering in through it as CAESAR's sofa is replaced by EVITA's sofa, bearing NELSON and KEISHA. She lies sideways facing us, head in her husband's lap as they idly watch TV on mute and talk…

WINDOW – TODAY

CAESAR: Okay…

EVITA: I never lied.

CAESAR: …you are a sly bitch.

EVITA: I never lied.

CAESAR: You said there was a man living with you.

EVITA: There is. That's a man, Caesar.

EVITA'S HOUSE

NELSON: Maradona.

KEISHA: No.

NELSON: Zidane.

KEISHA: No.

NELSON: Pele.

KEISHA: No.

Enter CHE, with snacks.

CHE: Beckham?

KEISHA: No footballers! He can't go round being called Beckham Ramsay.

CHE moves KEISHA's feet and squeezes onto the sofa.

CHE: S'no stupider 'n Nelson Ramsay.

NELSON: Che bruv – 'Maradona' Ramsay!

CHE: … Sounds like the bollocks to me.

KEISHA: Not 'The' bollocks, just bollocks. What if he doesn't like football?

CHE and NELSON look at each other.

NELSON / CHE: You what?

KEISHA: What if he likes ice-skating?

NELSON / CHE: Ice skating?!!!

KEISHA: You don't know – he might wanna be a ballet dancer…you never know!   CHE: Okay… She has lost it…

NELSON: I know. He ain't a ballet dancer.

CHE: (*Amused.*) Heh, heh, heh… 'Ballet dancer'.

NELSON: I felt him kick. That ain't no ballet dancer.

KEISHA: Have you felt a ballet dancer kick? You're not gonna be that kind of dad are you?

NELSON: What kind of dad?

KEISHA: Nothing.

NELSON: What kind of dad?

KEISHA: Forget it.

CHE: Heh, heh, heh! Ballet dancer!

THE WINDOW – 24 YEARS AGO

EVITA: (*Jumping up.*) I can't see!

CAESAR: Shut up, man!

EVITA: I can't hear! What they doing? What they saying?

CAESAR: I dunno – you're making too much noise. They're watching TV.

EVITA: Your dad?

CAESAR: And some lady, yeah… They're on the settee with the lights off. She's got her head in his lap. She's pregnant.

EVITA: What's pregnant?

CAESAR: Never mind.

EVITA: What's pregnant?

CAESAR: Shhh!

EVITA: I wanna see!

CAESAR: Shush, man! Okay – piggy back – one minute.

CAESAR helps EVITA climb on his back.

EVITA: Ohhhh! She's pretty, man!

CAESAR: Shut up, yeah?

EVITA: Is she your dad's sister?

CAESAR: I don't think so.

EVITA: They're watching telly just like us – she's lying on him just like us.

CAESAR: I think they're wearing wedding rings.

EVITA: So your Daddy ain't Mummy's husband?

CAESAR: No.

EVITA: Is my Daddy Mummy's husband?

CAESAR: I doubt it.

EVITA: Is anyone? What's wrong with her tummy?

CAESAR: She's pregnant.

EVITA: Oh. Okay. Does it hurt? Caese? Caesar, man, you alright?

CAESAR: (*Gently.*) Come down now, yeah? Nothing more to see.

EVITA'S PLACE – TODAY

KEISHA: … Richard.

NELSON: 'Richard'??

KEISHA: It's a king's name.

NELSON: Richard?

CHE: Heh, heh, heh…

KEISHA: It even means rule-hard.

NELSON: As in Dick for short?

CHE: Dick! Heh, heh, heh…

KEISHA: As in Rick.

NELSON: As in Dickie.

CHE: Dickie! Heh, heh, heh…

KEISHA: As in Lionheart…

CHE: … 'Little Dickie'!

KEISHA: (*Kicking CHE.*) } { CHE: Ow!
    Richard the Lionheart.

NELSON: What do you mean, 'that kind of dad'?

KEISHA: Oh Gosh…

NELSON: What did you mean, Keish?

KEISHA: I don't know, ignore me, I'm pregnant.

CHE: You heard the lady – ignore her.

KEISHA: Hormones have hijacked my brain…

CHE: Heh, heh, her, the whore…moans…

NELSON: What kind of dad?

KEISHA: Like yours. Narrow. The kind that 'just knows that it's a boy' the kind that'd sulk if that boy was a girl and kick off if that boy was gay.

CHE: That's every kind of dad.

NELSON: That's every kind of dad.

KEISHA: That's your kind of dad.

NELSON: You don't know him, Keish.

KEISHA: What?

NELSON: You don't know him. You've only see one side of him when he's under pressure. He ain't always like that.

KEISHA: Only when other people dare to speak up.

NELSON: He taught me to always speak up.

KEISHA: Just not to him…sha.

NELSON: You what?

KEISHA: My name's Kei*sha*. You make me sound like…

NELSON: …a cheesy tart?

NELSON high-fives with CHE, then grins at KEISHA and winks. KEISHA looks at him a moment, then gets up and walks off – we see that she is about five months pregnant…

Keisha, man!

CHE: Let her cool down, bredren, match is starting, anyway.

NELSON: I'm only pulling your chain! Keisha, man!

KEISHA: (*Already offstage.*) I'm not your man!!

NELSON: (*To himself.*) Oh, man! Again! (*To CHE.*) Dude, what the fuck?

CHE: (*Burps.*) What?

NELSON: What the fuck is wrong with her? This ain't marriage, this is…

CHE / NELSON: … Lion taming…

CHE: … She's pregnant, man – it's like she's on a nine-month period. You think it's bad now, wait till the baby. If you're lucky it'll be a girl and there'll be two of 'em.

NELSON sits silent.

… You alright, bruv?

NELSON: I'm working at fucking Top Shop all week and Blockbuster on weekends, I ain't spoke to my old man in nearly five months and my bird turned into a bitch what needs a muzzle. What do you think? I'm fucking sweet, geezer.

CHE: Alright, man! Slay me with sarcasm, why doncha! I never shagged Psycho-Yattie and knocked her up, did I? At least you can get a job.

NELSON: You can get a job?

CHE: Oh, man don't start – you know I'm allergic. What? It's a life threatening condition! You miss him, then?

NELSON: Who?

CHE: Your dad. Watching the match with him. Hanging out with him. Asking him for advice and that.

NELSON: I never asked him for advice.

CHE: He just gave it you anyway.

They smile. CHE sighs...

... I miss him.

Enter DEANNA, breathless in body-hugging exercise outfit.

NELSON: Mum!

CHE: (*Eyes on stalks.*) Dee!

DEANNA: Alright, babes?

CHE: I'm great, babes...

NELSON: Mum – You're early.

DEANNA: I'm proper gutted babes, Bloody aerobics class got cancelled so I went for a short run instead! I'm cream-crackered – Don't worry, you won't know I'm here – D'you want a sandwich and a protein shake?

KEISHA: (*Offstage.*) I AIN'T YOUR FUCKING BOY!

CHE: Got any raw meat?

KEISHA: (*Offstage.*) AND I'M NO-ONE'S FLIPPIN' QUICHE!!

DEANNA: Nelson! You never called her...

NELSON: It was a joke. It's fine – I'll talk to her.

DEANNA: She's pregnant, love –

NELSON: I had noticed mum… } { DEANNA: My advice, don't talk… just…

NELSON / DEANNA: ..listen…

NELSON: … Yeah, yeah, I think I know how to handle my own wife, mum…

DEANNA: She's very hormonal right now…

NELSON: Duh!

DEANNA: … The slightest thing'll set her off…

NELSON: Mum! I'm handling it! And you're ruining my concentration. Don't get involved, alright? Just put some clothes on and go out somewhere, yeah?

DEANNA: Give me five minutes – you won't even know I'm here. If you need me I'm in the kitchen.

They start to exit in different directions.

NELSON: I don't need you, mum!

CHE: Can we have cheese toasties?

NELSON: With turkey, yeah, I need the protein. (*Calling out.*) Keisha! (*To DEANNA.*) You were running down the street like that?

DEANNA rolls her eyes as they make their exits.

CHE: (*Eyes misting dreamily.*) She was running down the street like that…

WINDOW – CONTINUOUS

CAESAR: She was running down the street like that?

EVITA: What's she supposed to wear?

CAESAR: Clothes!! Where's she running like that, half nekkid and nipples to the wind?

EVITA: Caesar.

CAESAR: Wild, that's where! The woman's running wild! What kind of a knocking-shop halfway-house are you running here?

EVITA: I'm trying to keep your family together, seeing as you can't be bothered.

CAESAR: I thought you said the man in your house was moving out?

EVITA: He is – in the morning. They've got a flat.

CAESAR: A flat?

EVITA: It's only council.

CAESAR: How can they afford a flat?

EVITA: You heard him – He's working two jobs.

CAESAR: That was just bollocks though, weren't it? Two jobs?… Nelson?

EVITA: Two Jobs Nelson, that's his street name

CAESAR: What about college?

EVITA: You're just determined to be unhappy, innit?

CAESAR: Don't say, innit, it's vulgar. How they supposed to get decent jobs without college? Oh I forgot, they don't do degrees in Grime – what use is Oxbridge to these dizzy little rascals?

EVITA: Keisha's still at college…

CAESAR: I'll bet she is – she ain't stupid.

EVITA'S LIVING ROOM – CONTINUOUS

KEISHA stomps in lugging a heavy suitcase...

NELSON: Keisha, babe, this is stupid.

KEISHA: STUPID???!!!

NELSON: Not you! This!

KEISHA: This is me! I'm stupid?

NELSON: No! (*Looking to CHE, who is playing with TV remote.*) Not Stupid...

CHE: ... Silly.

NELSON: Silly! You are just being just a little bit silly. I only called you Keish, for gosh sakes. I was being affectionate, man!

CHE: (*Warning...*) She's not your man, bruv...

KEISHA: (*To CHE.*) Shut up! (*To NELSON.*) I'm not your man.

NELSON: I know!

KEISHA: I'm not one of your boys!

NELSON: I know!

KEISHA: I am the mother of your child.

NELSON: (*Sighing.*) I know...

KEISHA: (*Darkly.*) You what?

NELSON: (*Nervously.*) What?

KEISHA: What do you mean?

NELSON: (*Trying to read her face.*) What do you mean, what do I mean?

KEISHA: What do you mean, 'I know'?

CHE: Ohhhh shit...

NELSON: I, I, I mean I know. You are the mother of my
child – I know.

KEISHA: What do you mean 'I know' in that tone of voice? 'I
know'…what do you mean 'I know'.

CHE: Anyone want a drink?

CHE hurries off to the kitchen…

Dee!

NELSON: Baby, you're getting a bit scary-crazy, now…

KEISHA: Who the hell do you think you're talking to? I ain't
your mother, you know…

DEANNA enters with a tray, unseen by KEISHA.

NELSON: Keisha…

KEISHA: I ain't a doormat   NELSON: Keisha, she's
alright? I ain't going   here…
through seventeen years   Keisha, she's *here…*
of putting up with it
'cause I'm grateful to
be getting black dick!
You're dealing with a
black woman now and
you better come correct
or it's on, nigger, you get
me?

NELSON: It's the hormones, mum.

KEISHA turns and sees DEANNA.

DEANNA: I made sandwiches and shakes. Proteins and
vitamins. Sorry. I'm interrupting. They're in the kitchen.
(*Turning.*) Sorry.

DEANNA leaves.

KEISHA: (*To NELSON.*) Thanks a lot.

She picks up the heavy case. NELSON steps forward to help…

Leave it.

She leaves, lugging the suitcase. NELSON stares after her for a moment.

NELSON: Go then!

He drops back onto the sofa, picks up the TV remote, starts to point it at the TV…then throws it down, sinking into sofa…

Muuuum!

WINDOW – CONTINUOUS

CAESAR: Well, well, well… Trouble in paradise… who'd have guessed? That was better than television!

CAESAR turns to go…

EVITA: Where you going?

CAESAR: Home. I'm hungry.

EVITA: Caesar!

CAESAR: What do you want me to do? He's a man – he's got a man's problems – he can handle 'em like a man!

EVITA: You know he can't.

CAESAR: Yeah, I know he can't – you know he can't. Now it's time he knew he can't.

EVITA: Don't you even wanna know what Deanna's got to say?

CAESAR: Who cares what she's got to say?

DEANNA comes in.

DEANNA: She gone?

CAESAR: (*Darting back to the window…*) What she say?

NELSON: I dunno. Whatever… She's gone, mum.

DEANNA: Why don't you go after her?

NELSON: I can't.

DEANNA: Why not?

NELSON: I dunno. I can't. She hates me.

DEANNA: She don't hate you.

NELSON: Yeah, she does. She hates me. You heard what she said.

DEANNA: She didn't say she hates you.

NELSON: She called me a nigger.

DEANNA: People always say the worst things to the ones they care for the most. Love makes you vulnerable. People struggle for balance and they say things so you feel the same lack of control that they feel. It's a compliment in a way… Like your dad – See how charming he is with people at work and at parties – strangers and acquaintances – and how he is with us? I know it feels like arrogance – but it ain't. It's his insecurity. It's his vulnerability. He's allowing us to see his angry, frightened, threatened side. 'Cause he knows we'll always love him no matter what, so he's safe.

NELSON: Yeah, but in the end he drove us away. Like I've driven Keish away. Just 'cause someone loves you don't mean they'll stick around no matter what.

DEANNA: Depends on the person. I'm still around, ain't I?

NELSON: Yeah, but you left dad. Even you ain't that much of a…

Pause.

DEANNA: …door mat?

NELSON: She's left me mum. What do I do?

DEANNA: Think about it – What would your dad have to do to make things better between him and you?

NELSON: Dunno.

DEANNA: Would sorry make a difference?

NELSON: Dad don't say sorry – his mouth ain't fixed that way.

DEANNA: And how's your mouth fixed?

NELSON: What have I got to be sorry about? I only called her Keish. Am I supposed to watch every word I say for the rest of my life, while she calls me whatever she wants whenever she feels like it? You walked out on Dad after eighteen years – She's walked out on me after eighteen weeks. Dad was right about her. Over her... I'm over her! (*Jumping up.*) Right!

DEANNA: You going after her?

NELSON: I'm going to the kitchen. I'm hungry.

DEANNA sinks back into the sofa.

CAESAR: Hmm. Maybe I under-estimated the boy... He might actually be waking himself up. Mmm, now I'm *really* hungry!

EVITA: You're happy with that mess?

CAESAR: I'm never happy, sis – I'm a dad.

EVITA: Dee needs you, Caesar. Look at her.

CAESAR: I've seen her. (*Not looking.*) I see her. I see her everywhere I look.

EVITA: Caesar...

CAESAR: She! Left me! They both left me! Everybody's where they chose to be, reaping what they've sown with no 'arrogant, insecure' man to treat 'em like doormats. If anyone needs me they know where I am... I'm right where they left me.

EVITA: Is that where you wanna be though?

24 YEARS AGO – CAESAR & EVITA'S BEDROOM

EVITA: What would you do if she never come home?

CAESAR: She is coming home. Shoes.

EVITA sits on the bed, while CAESAR takes her shoes off.

EVITA: What if she don't though?

CAESAR: She is though.

EVITA: You wouldn't care anyway. You'd be happy. You'd go and live with your dad and your new mum happily ever after.

CAESAR: She's not my new mum. Socks.

EVITA struggles to take her socks off.

I've never even met her. She's probably never even heard of me. She probably never will.

EVITA: You think he'll stay with her forever and ever?

CAESAR: I don't know.

EVITA: I do. He won't stay. I'm never getting married.

CAESAR: Don't be silly. Come here.

He whips his sister's socks off and curls one into each shoe.

EVITA: I ain't. Can brothers and sisters get married?

CAESAR: No!

EVITA: Then I'm never getting married.

CAESAR: You're mad… In..!

He lifts the duvet and deftly swivels her in and under.

EVITA: I hope Mum never comes back.

CAESAR removes his shoes and gets on the bed…

CAESAR: Don't talk stupid.

EVITA: I do. I hope she never comes back and you can adopt me and take me to school and pick me up and make me dinner every day and tell me stories. I'm never gonna grow up and I'm never gonna get married and you can look after me forever and ever.

CAESAR: You don't want mum to come back?

EVITA: I do really… But not till she's grown up.

CAESAR: Beat box!

EVITA and CAESAR beat-box together. CAESAR laughs.

EVITA: (*Embarrassed.*) What?

CAESAR: It's cute! Don't stop!

> *Once upon a Whatever, yeah, back in the day*
> *There was a little girl coming up in Forest Gate*
> *Dreamed of somehow someday finding a way*
> *Of making her escape up and outta the estate*
> *So, she plotted, she planned, she scratched and she schemed*
> *She bided her time till she finally growed*
> *Tall enough to reach and seize her big dreams*
> *Then she took to the stage with her riddims and her flows*
> *And her father appears in the midst of the crowd*
> *To stand side by side with her growed-up mother*
> *To holler and cheer proper loud proper proud*
> *But the loudest of the shouting come from her big brother*

Phone rings.

I'm busy!

> *So all you babes dreaming down in the hood*
> *Living so far away from your goal*
> *Get your sleep practise hard and be good*
> *And you will grow to be star of the show…*

93

Yes, you will grow to be the star of the Mofo show!

EVITA: I will grow to be the star of my *mofo show*!

CAESAR / EVITA: (*Theatrical fake collapse on the bed.*) *We out!*

Phone rings.

CAESAR wakes up.

CAESAR: (*Waking up.*) Shit!

CAESAR wakes from his sleep to answer his phone…

Go to hell.

Light up on CHE – on the phone.

CHE: Yo Caesar!

CAESAR: Che? You mad? It's three in the morning.

CHE: You need to come down the police station, man – and bring your cheque book, yeah?

CAESAR: I'm on my way… What's the offence?

CHE: Drunk and disorderly – Breach of the peace – resisting arrest…

CAESAR: (*Chuckling.*) Boy, you been *busy*!

CHE: Not me! Nelson!

CAESAR: Nelson?

CHE: I tried to calm him down but he was on one, man!

CAESAR: Nelson?

CHE: He was out of control.

CAESAR: Nelson?

CHE: Nelson, man! Your Nelson!

CAESAR: Ain't my Nelson, sorry.

CHE: Caesar.

CAESAR: Call his mum.

CHE: His mum?

CAESAR: Sorry, his mate…

CHE: Dee?

CAESAR: His mate, your mate – everyone's mate, Dee the door-mat – give her a bell and she'll be there in a flash with cocoa and snacks. If you need me, I'll be asleep.

CHE: Caesar, man!

CAESAR hangs up. He lies down. Can't sleep.

CAESAR: Shit.

CAESAR jumps up.

24 YEARS AGO

PRECIOUS appears. She is drunk.

PRECIOUS: Caesar?

CAESAR: Mum?

PRECIOUS: Caesar baby…

PRECIOUS staggers towards him…

Where are you, darlin?

CAESAR grabs PRECIOUS, just as her legs give way…

CAESAR: Here! (*holding her.*) Here I am, mum.

PRECIOUS: Here you are, my baby… my first born… Come here, dance with me! *'Red Red wi-iine! Goes to my head.'*

CAESAR: I'll make you some coffee.

PRECIOUS: No coffee! Dance with mummy!

CAESAR: Mum, Vita's sleeping.

PRECIOUS: Oh, my baby girl... where is she? Evita, darlin!!!!

She heads towards the bed, CAESAR steers away...

CAESAR: No, no, Precious darlin'! Let's dance yeah?

PRECIOUS: (*Dancing with him.*) Yeaaah man! (*Hugging him very tight.*) Oh, my first born, my little man... *'Red Red Wine – Goes to my head...'* I wanted a girl you know, I wanted a little princess to take after me. I said to the doctor – don't tell me – you don't have to tell me – I know it's a girl. But you slid out and they held you up and I saw your little pee-pee and I thought, 'awwww! Bless him... My first born...' I love my little Evita – my beautiful baby girl, but there's no-one so special as your first born... I'm glad I kept you. What would I do without you, eh? Where would we be? Lost is where I'd be...you're the reason I come home... you're the reason I bother to have a home. My little man... Without you I'd be an orphan. Your grandma never understood me. Never loved me, never liked me, never did, never will. No brothers no sisters? What's that about? We're West Indian! Where's my six brothers and sisters? She stopped having kids to spite me. Because she hated me – 'Cause she was ashamed. Where's all my uncles and aunties and my hundred cousins? She kept me away from everyone like a guilty mistake and then she wondered why I pulled up my skirts and ran as fast as I can...to you... You're my only family. When you were born, they told me, you know, they sat me down with adoption papers and they said 'You're too young, you're too loose, you're not ready...' But I knew – It weren't about me... Little Caesar was ready. You were special, you were what was missing in the world. And I had to have you. Weren't easy, Gave up drinking spirits – gave up smoking. Nibbled hash cookies for seven months – kept me lungs clear specially. 'Specially for my baby boy. Only went out at weekends – and bank holidays... and every other Wednesday...but you were worth every sacrifice. *'Red Red wine… Stay close to me…don't let me be alone…'*

CAESAR: Who sat you down?

PRECIOUS: Mmm?

CAESAR: Who wanted me adopted?

PRECIOUS: Your grandma, your dad, passing strangers – everybody… 'Cept me. I knew. You were meant to come and change the world a little bit. I knew. And here you are. (*Blinking at him blearily.*) What you doing up? You got school in the morning.

CAESAR: So have you.

PRECIOUS: Sod that – I ain't going in.

CAESAR: You have to – you've spent the grant money!

PRECIOUS: Don't you tell me what to do! I'm a big woman! I'm a grown up big woman of 27 and I'm too old to be a student and I'm too old for homework and I'm too old for you to be looking at me like that!

PRECIOUS slaps CAESAR.

Don't look at me like that! Can't a gyal go out once in while and be young? I'm old enough to be as young as I like… Why you got to look at me? Take off that face, alright? That's your Dad's face! You gonna take after him? You gonna run away and leave me as well, are you? You think I'm stupid? You think I'm stupid? You're stupid, if you think I'm stupid. Look at you, your big black stupid face, looking at me. You're just waiting, ain't you? Just counting! Six more years – six more years…

PRECIOUS: (*Shoving him.*) Go then! Go now! Go on! Piss off! Go! } { CAESAR: Mum!

PRECIOUS: You're gonna go anyway! Why waste time! Go!

CAESAR: You're gonna wake up Vita!

She pushes him to the front door –

PRECIOUS: … Go now!

CAESAR: Mum! Mum, please! I got no shoes on!

PRECIOUS shoves CAESAR out and slams the door.

PRECIOUS: Sssh! You'll wake up your sister!

CAESAR: Mum!

CAESAR wanders away from the door, he step on something sharp.

Ahhh! Mum! Nana Grace!

24 YEARS AGO – NANA GRACE'S HOUSE

CAESAR is crying…

CAESAR: Nana Grace..!

NANA GRACE appears in her robe, brandishing a baseball bat.

NANA GRACE: Is who dat? Don't make me use the bat, y'know!

CAESAR: It's Caesar.

NANA GRACE: Wait, boy, I'm indecent! Turn round, make I fix me wig and teeth!

CAESAR turns away, while NANA GRACE grabs her wig and teeth.

CAESAR: Sorry Nana Grace. I know it's the middle of the night… I didn't know where else to go.

NANA GRACE: Is wha' that nasty lickle bitch done now?

Wig fixed, she turns back and peers at him.

Where your shoes? Bwoy, you crying?

CAESAR nods…

Ohhhh! Come here, baby! (*Opening her arms.*) Come to Nana Grace.

CAESAR is enveloped in NANA GRACE's embrace…

My lickle man! Did Mama make you cry…? Nana understands… Mama makes Nana cry all the time… Are you hungry? Nana made rice and peas!

CAESAR: She hates me, Nana Grace.

NANA GRACE: Nah, baby, mama don't hate you… Mama's just young. You want chicken? Nana made chicken!

CAESAR: You should hear what she say, Nana, ⎱⎰ NANA GRACE: I know baby…

CAESAR: you should see what she does. ⎱⎰ NANA GRACE: I know baby… You want some punch?

CAESAR: (*Pushing her away.*) You don't know!! You don't know what she like!

NANA GRACE heads to the fridge.

NANA GRACE: I know exactly what she's like, baby… She's like me.

CAESAR: She's not like you! She can't even cook! She had a baby when she was seventeen! You were thirty!

NANA GRACE: But I wasn't ready. I wasn't ready. I thought I was ready. I'd been an abiding child and a God-Fearing girl, I thought I'd become a wise and ready woman. I came to this country to escape my family and find my dream. I was lonely, it was cold – and in the long dark evenings, I stumbled. And fell straight under a man. Under his body, under his spell. I thought I was in love. Maybe I was. He was so handsome, so gentlemanly, so kind – I thought 'Jesus won't mind' and I lay with him. And one morning the gentle man was gently gone. And then there we were, your mama and me in this cold cold place. And I wasn't ready. I thought all a child needed was food and shelter and school and licks. If I worked hard and was righteous and prayed that would be enough. But children need more. I know that now. Children need more than love, more than food. Children need passion. But I believed that I owed my faith to the Lord and your mama's father had run away with all the passion. And there was none left for the child I had named Precious. So I fed her and made her big – bwoy, that gyal got big – schooled her with licks and I told myself that she should feel loved. But without a sense of passion there is no feeling of love. And without that anchor of faith she drifted – just like me – only younger. I told her she wasn't ready. I warned her you'd grow up bad, just like she did. She swore to me you wouldn't. And you didn't. She did well. Not perfect, but well. But I think she missed something – I think she missed showing you the love. She loves you, little Caesar – with a passion – She's just lost, like her mama was and like you will be someday. But give her time and she will find you.

CAESAR: You're so wise, Nana Grace. And you cook so good. Why can't we live here with you?

NANA GRACE: Because your mama needs you, little man – to make her wise, like she made me. One day you will forgive her. Meanwhile, you must watch over the family like you've been doing and keep everyone safe. That's your calling – to be the first man in our family that never ran away.

CAESAR: So I'm supposed to be a Man, when I ain't even been a kid, yet.

NANA GRACE: I know – it's a burden – but it's who you are. Kids are everywhere. Real grown men are special. You're special, little man. You'll see. Now, finish your ackee and we're gonna lay you down – And in the morning Nana's gonna walk you home.

CAESAR: No. I should go home now. You go back to bed. Thanks, Nana Grace.

NANA GRACE: Make sure you take some dumplings with you. (*Digging in the fridge.*) And some for your baby sister…

CAESAR: Nana Grace… Why's it all so hard?

NANA GRACE: I don't know. It never gets easier. And it never get easier to understand. But somehow, in the end, everything is always alright.

She holds out a bag of food.

CAESAR: Thanks. I'm not hungry.

CAESAR turns and starts to walk home…

NANA GRACE: Caesar.

CAESAR turns back.

It'll be alright.

CAESAR walks into…

POLICE STATION LOBBY – TODAY

CHE sits on a long wooden bench, texting…

CAESAR: Alright?

CHE: (*Not looking up.*) Alright…you said you weren't coming…

CAESAR: I was in the area.

CHE: … Cool…

Enter DEANNA in a sexy outfit, flipping her phone closed and immediately texting…

DEANNA: Right, that's sorted! Taxi's outside. Let's get the silly little bugger… (*Brushing past CAESAR.*) 'scuse me… (*Texting.*) …home.

CAESAR: (*Drily.*) Excuse me.

DEANNA: Che said you weren't coming.

CAESAR: I was in the area.

DEANNA: Okay… Where's your shoes?

CAESAR looks down at his bare feet.

CAESAR: Nice dress, new?

DEANNA: (*Still texting.*)…old.

CAESAR: How comes I've never seen it?

DEANNA: You tell me.

Enter EVITA, propping up a drunken NELSON with one arm and texting with another.

NELSON: Mum? Where's mum, I love you mum!

DEANNA: (*Still texting.*) I know!

NELSON: I love you Aunty Evita!

EVITA: (*Still texting.*) I know…

NELSON: I love you Che, mate!

CHE: I know.

NELSON sees CAESAR.

CAESAR: Alright?

NELSON stares for a moment, then lifts a hand to his mouth and pukes violently through his fingers.

EVITA: Oh for God's sake!   DEANNA: Nelson, you
Take your child woman!   mucky pup…

DEANNA: Charming…

CHE: (*Shaking his foot.*) Dude! These trainers are new!!

CAESAR: … Come here, you stupid little skid-mark…

Both DEANNA and EVITA are already manoeuvring NELSON to sit on the bench, both still texting… CAESAR tries to get in there but there's no room…

DEANNA: Come here, babe, let mummy hold you... (*To CAESAR.*) I've got him, Caesar, you'll only make him chuck up again... (*To NELSON.*) You daft git, you know you can't hold your drink...

} {

EVITA: Auntie's got you – don't puke on auntie, yeah? Here, you go – head between your legs, yeah? (*To CAESAR.*) I've got him (*To NELSON.*) You know you can't hold nothing stronger than fizzy water...

KEISHA bursts in, heavily pregnant. Everyone looks at her.

KEISHA: Where is he?

NELSON takes a breath, then stands up and faces KEISHA.

NELSON: Hey you.

KEISHA: Hey you.

NELSON: You look bigger.

KEISHA: I am bigger. It's been a month.

NELSON: I know. It's been brutal.

KEISHA: And I've been pregnant.

NELSON: And I've been worrying.

KEISHA: And I've been waiting.

NELSON: And I've been stupid.

KEISHA: And I'm still waiting.

NELSON: And I'm still...

NELSON looks around at everyone listening.

KEISHA: ...still...?

NELSON: ...still...

NELSON sees CAESAR staring at him, turns back to KEISHA decisively.

…sorry. I'm sorry. Very very sorry… So so so so so so sorry. And the father of your kid, er, child… And I will never desert my wife or kid or kick my kid out or raise a hand to him…er, her. Or raise my voice to her – or you – And I love you and I'm here for you. And I'm sorry.

KEISHA: Aww, baby…!

They float into each other's arms…

NELSON: Baby… (*Gently bumping into her tummy.*) Shit! (*To tummy.*) Sorry, baby…

KEISHA: It's okay, he's just glad to see you again…

NELSON: And I've missed him. (*Kiss.*) And his mum. (*Kiss.*) Her mum. (*Kiss.*) Their mum.

CHE: Can we go before I throw up?

DEANNA: Bugger! I forgot! (*Texting.*) I've got a cab waiting!

ALL: 'Cab'!

KEISHA: You only live down the road!

DEANNA: I was at Da Klub.

ALL: 'Da Klub'?!

CHE: With who?

NELSON: (*Meaning CAESAR.*) Not with him?

EVITA: Girl, are you on a date?

NELSON / CHE / KEISHA: A date?!

DEANNA: No!

CHE: With who?

DEANNA: I'm not on a date!

KEISHA: Oh, my God, you are totally on a date!

DEANNA: I am not on a date!

NELSON: You're on a fucking date? Mum!

DEANNA: I'm just out for a dance.

CHE: Is that what they're calling it now?

NELSON: Shut up, bred.

DEANNA: I just wanted to go out and forget about everything.

NELSON: (*Horrified.*) As in me?

CHE: (*Hopeful.*) As in me?

DEANNA: As in me. I just wanted to forget myself.

CHE: With who? (*Prompting NELSON.*) Bredren, with who?

DEANNA: … A friend.

NELSON: 'A friend'?

Enter PRECIOUS.

PRECIOUS: You heard her, you ain't deaf. You lot coming or what? Any longer and it'll be cheaper to buy the cab.

CAESAR: (*Turning to DEANNA.*) 'A Friend'?

PRECIOUS: (*Spotting NELSON.*) Oh, is that my baby, grandson? Nelsie!!! You alright, darlin'? Give Nana a kiss… (*Catching a whiff of NELSON's breath.*) Never mind, darlin'… (*Pops a mint in his mouth.*) Have a mint. Boy, how you so thin! My house for breakfast, I'll make Bulla cake. (*Spotting CHE.*) Is that who I think it is, all grown up and handsomely chavtastic?

CHE: Hello, Mrs Ramsay.

PRECIOUS: Miss. But you can call me Precious. (*To CAESAR.*) You look like shit. When was the last time you creamed your foot then? Put on your shoes!

NELSON: Thanks for paying my on the spot fine, Nana Precious.

PRECIOUS: Thats what Nanas are for, darlin? Right! We all going back down Da Klub, then? It's time to make sure that baby gets some rhythm! As my wise ol' bitch of a mother you used to say – 'Let's step on the good foot!'

PRECIOUS takes CHE's arm and leads him off…

You know how to whine and grine, boy? Or you need mama to school you?

DEANNA: You coming Evita, babe?

EVITA: I don't know, babe… Da Klub? I'm in my nightie!

DEANNA: Never stopped you before…

EVITA: … True.

PRECIOUS: Thats my baby! (*To DEANNA.*) You do something with her hair, I'll have a go at the face, (*Pulling out make-up.*) Maybe we can fix up her up a man…

EVITA: One hour! I've got work in the morning.

NELSON: (*To KEISHA.*) You wanna go dancing or you wanna go home? I mean to yours?

KEISHA: Ours.

They smile.

Well, you know it might be our last chance…dance-wise…

NELSON: (*Moving in, smiling…*) And we are gonna be somewhat occupied soon.

CHE: How 'bout you, Mr Ramsay?

CAESAR: Me?

CHE: Fancy checking out Da Klub? Maybe a little MC rematch?

CAESAR: Me? Looking like shit?

DEANNA: Caesar…

CAESAR: You heard my loving supportive mother – I look like shit. You think she wants to be seen out raving with me? Her dirty little secret? Proof of her real age and reminder of her slutty teenage mistakes?

DEANNA: Caesar!

PRECIOUS: Is who you calling a slut?

EVITA: Caesar, you're out of order.

CAESAR: You think I want to be seen out with her? The woman that left me alone night after night child-minding her precious baby daughter? The pot-head that drank and toked away my childhood? The treacherous old crone what told me licks would pull my family together then sat back and watched it fall apart? All so she could sweep in and play the glam granny that everyone loves? But I'm sure she's already told you, Nelson – that your precious Nana Precious was the one what instructed me to give you licks?

EVITA: Caesar, leave it! } { DEANNA: Right that's it, we're going – everyone in the cab.

CAESAR: That when you were kids your Nana used to call little Che here that pikey poor boy and advised me not to let you two play together?

No-one moves.

And obviously your New Best Friend has told you, Dee, that she wanted me to force you down the abortion clinic and then get shot of you – but of course she's told you – She's lovely, open, honest Nana Precious – everyone's friend! All is forgiven and youre all going dancing with her, like she ain't the Devil and all this ain't a hell of her making. Do you know what the word slut actually means? Derived from the word slattern – it means lazy, it means messy, it means sloppy, it means cheap. Did I say I used to hate you? Sorry, mummy, I lied. I still hate you. I've never stopped hating you. And nothing is forgiven and nothing ever can be. And I will never go out dancing with you. Why? Because I! Am not a slut!

No-one moves.

What you gonna do now, Mama Precious? Give me licks?

PRECIOUS turns away. Slowly she leaves, vulnerable and suddenly old.

DEANNA: (*Heartbroken.*) Oh Caesar...

DEANNA leaves and catches up with PRECIOUS, puts her arms around her. CHE turns to go.

CAESAR: No exit line, Che?

CHE stops – does not look round...

CAESAR: Not even a heartbreaking 'Oh Caesar'? How about, 'this is one of those times when you're glad you ain't got a dad'?

NELSON: How about, 'This is one of the those times when I wish I didn't'?

NELSON holds his hand out. KEISHA takes it. KEISHA raises a finger.

CAESAR: Yes?

KEISHA shakes her head. KEISHA and NELSON leave. CHE is still there, staring at the ground.

Still miss me, man?

CHE: Yeah... I still miss you, man.

He looks round, his eyes full of tears.

CHE leaves.

EVITA and CAESAR are left alone.

CAESAR: So I'm out of order am I? So you're taking her side an all. Come Sis, you know what she was like. You remember. Why should we just forgive her and let her get away with it?

EVITA: Because she was just a kid. Why did you freak out about Nelson becoming a dad? Because he's just a kid.

CAESAR: When you have a kid, you forfeit being a kid yourself. That's the moment when you have to grow up whether you like it or not. You were the one who said you'd never get married or have kids because of her. You were the one who never wanted her to come home.

EVITA: I was a kid, Caesar.

CAESAR: Why'd you never get married, then? Why'd you never have kids, yourself?

EVITA: Hold up, I ain't on the scrap heap yet, you know. Why ain't I had kids yet? Because I'm scared. I'm scared I'll do what Deanna done and find an amazing one-in-a-million-man who becomes an angry fascist who'll turn his back on his family when he don't get his own way. Because I ain't been lucky like you – finding someone special to share my life with, who'll put up with all my bullshit. I ain't alone through choice, Caesar – that's your story. But imagine this, yeah – What if, God forbid, you're wrong? What if growing up isn't something you do when you have kids yourself. What if growing is what you do when you finally forgive your parents? What if your problem ain't that you're a dad, what if your problem is that you're a dad that's still a kid? Eh?

EVITA leaves. CAESAR is left alone.

SEVENTEEN YEARS AGO – CAESAR AND DEANNA'S COUNCIL FLAT

CAESAR leans over the cot. Hissing loudly.

CAESAR: Dee!

Enter DEANNA, exhausted.

DEANNA: What?

CAESAR: Shh!

DEANNA: What?

CAESAR listens to the baby.

CAESAR: Dee!

DEANNA: What!

CAESAR: He ain't breathing!

DEANNA: What?

CAESAR: He's stopped! He's stopped breathing. I was watching him sleeping and he just…

DEANNA: What are you on, about? Caesar, calm down… I can't hear him… Caesar! Shush!

CAESAR shushes. They listen.

Sound FX: Baby sigh.

DEANNA and CAESAR breathe again.

CAESAR: He's fine.

DEANNA: Of course he's fine.

CAESAR: Why's he so quiet? He's a Ramsay! It ain't natural! Evita weren't quiet. She never shut up!

DEANNA: Maybe we should get some sleep while he's still quiet.

CAESAR: In a bit, yeah? I'm just watching him. Look at him, man. How'd this happen? Where'd all this come from? Everything's there…look at the tiny fingernails…

DEANNA: …and teeny tiny eyelashes…

CAESAR: Can you believe this great big thing come out the little hole at the end of my dick?

DEANNA: (*Laughs, nudging him.*) Oy!

CAESAR: You done your bit. You done good. I cried watching you, you know. I was supposed to film everything. But I couldn't see through the viewfinder – I couldn't stop shaking. What you went through – what you did... You're amazing, you know that?

DEANNA: I'm knackered, I know that much.

They stand entwined, watching the baby.

CAESAR: Youre right – you should go to bed. I'll be there in a bit.

DEANNA: Ohhh...! You know I can't sleep without you.

CAESAR: You're not without me. I'm just here.

DEANNA watches CAESAR watching her son... She smiles.

DEANNA: We can't watch him for ever, babes.

CAESAR: Why not?

DEANNA leaves. CAESAR looks at his baby.

You know doncha, Nelson, my bredren? Im always watching you, yeah? Always here for you, no matter what. 'Cause I'm your dad, yeah? Look, Nana Grace...hes got your eyes.

NOW – GRAVEYARD

CAESAR at NANA GRACE's grave.

CAESAR: Nana Grace, I've failed. I tried so hard to be the man who stayed that I drove everyone away. I've given my life to being a good husband and father – provided food and a home – tried to be solid – and here I am – another absent father and my woman's another single mother. Do you hate me too, Nana Grace? Are you disappointed? Im sorry Nana Grace.

Enter PRECIOUS holding flowers.

PRECIOUS: Boy, why you have to talk stupid?

They stand looking at each other, awkwardly...

CAESAR: Why would your Nana be disappointed in you?
Let's face it, everyone else is.

PRECIOUS: Speak for yourself.

CAESAR: I am.

PRECIOUS moves towards the grave.

PRECIOUS: Lord Jesus, Mama Grace, this child knows how
to feel sorry for himself, ain't it? Anyone who saw you
together knows you could never be disappointed in your
baby Caesar. You were too busy being disappointed in me.
I'm sorry, Mama Grace. I'm sorry I wasn't a better mother.
But I tried.

CAESAR: She knows.

PRECIOUS: Does she?

CAESAR: She told me she thought you'd done a good job.

PRECIOUS: Yeah? (*Looking at him.*) She's right. She's always
right... The bitch. You miss her bad, innit?

CAESAR nods.

... Me too, baby...me too. You have her eyes.

CAESAR: You too.

CAESAR starts to cry. PRECIOUS strokes him awkwardly...

PRECIOUS: Ohhhh, my baby! My baby boy! Mamas got you!
(*Attempting to embrace him.*) Boy, how you get so damn big?
Here.

*She sits on a nearby bench, she indicates her lap. CAESAR looks at
her.*

Come to Mama Precious.

CAESAR lays down and rests his head on her lap.

Okay?

CAESAR: (*Big shuddering breath.*) Okay...

CAESAR starts to cry.

PRECIOUS: Yes, baby, you cry – cry all you want...all over Mama Precious's freshly dry-cleaned jeans, it's cool... Mama's here... Mama's here...

CAESAR's tears subside.

There you go. Ain't that better? Here...

PRECIOUS hands CAESAR a handkerchief. He noisily blows his nose. He hands it back. Attempting graciousness, PRECIOUS takes it gingerly by the corner, then tosses it into a nearby bin.

CAESAR: ... Mum... Am I like my Dad? Do I look like him? Talk like him? Act like him?

PRECIOUS: You have a look of him. There are flashes of him. But you take more after me...and your Nana.

CAESAR: Do you miss him? Do you wish he'd stayed? Do you ever wonder how things would have been?

PRECIOUS: I'm too busy dealing with things as they are. They'd have been different. I wouldn't have had your sister. I used to think maybe if you'd had a dad, if I'd had a dad, we wouldn't have had a kid so young. But it didn't stop Nelson. Nothings as simple as we'd like it to be. Do you regret having him?

CAESAR: I should, shouldn't I?

PRECIOUS: You should, yeah.

CAESAR: Do you regret having me?

PRECIOUS: Boy, you mad? Look at you. Young or not, wild or not, I still did a hell of a job. Do I miss your dad? Or mine? You can't miss what you never had. I miss you.

CAESAR: I miss Nelson.

PRECIOUS: You don't have to. Just like you don't have to do what I did and make all your Nana's mistakes. You can break the chain and become a good parent before you become a a good grandparent. There's still time.

CAESAR stares at her.

…just. Go.

CAESAR: I should go. I have to go… Sorry Nana Grace – I have to go.

PRECIOUS: Wait.

She hands his the flowers.

You'll need these.

CAESAR: Thanks mum.

He starts to go.

PRECIOUS: Wait!

She pops some food into his mouth.

I made you some bulla cake… Go.

OUTSIDE EVITA'S HOUSE

CAESAR beats on the door…

CAESAR: Deanna..! Deanna…! DEE!

DEANNA comes running to the door in a fluster, pulling on her shoes.

DEANNA: Oh my God, oh my God, oh my God, oh my God…

She opens the door – she and CAESAR stare at each other, breathless.

Caesar, what are you doing here?

CAESAR: I'm sorry. I should have listened. I should have sat down with you and talked and listened and we should have dealt with everything – You, me, our kid – our son, his girl – his wife…together. I shouldn't have panicked, I shouldn't have shouted and I shouldn't have let you go. I should've have kept it together – I should have kept us together – I should have married you…years ago. I should have married you, Dee – a thousand times over. We should be married. Marry me – please marry me a thousand times and we'll sort every thing out together. It's not too late. Will you marry me?… Please. (*Looking at her.*) What do you mean, what am I doing here? What do you mean, 'Caesar'? Who were you expecting? Richard Gere?

DEANNA: I mean, I just… Who called you?

CAESAR: (*Looking at her dishevelment.*) Am I interrupting something?

CHE runs in. Gasping to the point of hyperventilation.

CHE: Dee! Dee!

CAESAR: This is interesting.

DEANNA: We're gonna need an ambulance!

CAESAR: Only one?

CHE: Mr Ramsay!

CHE hurls himself at CAESAR.

Thank you, God!

CAESAR: (*Puzzled.*) You can call me Caesar…

DEANNA: Oh, for Christ's sake!

She pulls CHE's phone from his pocket and tries to dial…

CHE runs off.

CHE: I'm coming mate!

CAESAR: That's flattering.

EVITA runs in, wearing her robe…

EVITA: Deanna, gal, what's taking you damn long?

CAESAR: Okay, now I'm really worried…

DEANNA: I'm trying to get this poxy phone to work! (*Calling after CHE.*) Che! How do you unlock this bloody thing?

EVITA: Gimme that!

DEANNA: Don't snatch! (*Snatching it back.*) It's rude!

EVITA: (*Snatching it back.*) What you expect, I'm a rude gal!

CHE and NELSON scurry in, carrying a screaming KEISHA.

KEISHA: AAAAAAAAAAA } { NELSON: Muuuuum!
AAAAAAAAAAHHHH
HHH!

DEANNA: What the hell are you doing? Put her down!

CHE & NELSON start to lower her to the ground.

Not like that! Stand her up!

KEISHA: No! I don't want to stand up!

KEISHA refuses to use her legs, NELSON struggles to hold her up from behind without crushing her bump.

EVITA: (*Struggling with the phone.*) Bluetooth, e-mail… Don't they make phones that just phone no more? (*Shoving the phone back at DEANNA.*) You try it, I'm fetching mine.

EVITA runs off.

DEANNA: Evita! Where you going?

EVITA: To panic!

DEANNA: (*To boys.*) Keep her up! Walk her round!

KEISHA: I don't want to walk around!

DEANNA: Keisha, you've got to keep moving!

KEISHA: I don't want to keep fucking moving! I want to fucking DIE!

CHE: Keesh, watch the baby, man!

KEISHA: (*Trying to kick him, while NELSON holds her back…*) FUCK THE BABY! And FUCK YOU! MY NAME ain't KEESH! and I AIN'T YOUR MAN!

DEANNA: (*Dropping phone.*) }{ CHE: Don't take it out on
Bollocks! me, you psychotic she-
wolf! I never knocked
you up!

KEISHA: (*Pausing and panting.*) You're right… (*Hitting NELSON.*) Bastard! You did this to me, you dirty randy bastard!!!! I! HATE! YOU! You are never touching me again! Never!

NELSON: Mum, she's hitting me! (*To CHE.*) Help us mate!

KEISHA: (*Hitting CHE.*) }{ CHE: You help me!
Don't! Touch! Me! Dee!

NELSON: Mum!

DEANNA: Keisha! You have got to calm down!

KEISHA: I don't want to }{ DEANNA: Che, how do you
calm down! I want this work this phone? We
thing out of my body! need an ambulance or
(*Lashing out at NELSON* a taxi!
and CHE.) Take it out,
you bastard! Make him
take it out! Out! Out!

CHE: Sod the ambulance! Call the psycho ward! She wants sectioning!

NELSON: Calm down baby! You're scaring me!

EVITA enters with phone.

117

EVITA: Found it – who do I call?

NELSON / CHE: 999!

EVITA: Oh shit!

KEISHA: (*To DEANNA.*) I'm sorry, I called you a doormat, Dee, you are not a doormat, you are a goddess!

EVITA: (*Carefully dialling.*)
...9...
...9...

KEISHA has a contraction, letting out a wail and goes onto all fours on the floor. She lets out an all mighty scream of pain as she does. EVITA, reacts to the scream by dropping the phone and doesn't finish dialing 999.

KEISHA: How the hell did you do this? How did you survive? Help me Dee! Help me!

Ambulance siren. Flashing light.

Everyone looks at EVITA.

DEANNA: How'd you do that?

EVITA: I didn't.

CAESAR: I did.

Everyone looks at CAESAR, holding his phone.

Che – fetch Keisha's stuff.

CHE runs off.

Keisha. Take Nelson's hand.

KEISHA takes NELSON's hand.

Nelson's gonna help you breathe. Nelson.

NELSON: I can't.

CAESAR: Yes, you can. Like in the classes.

NELSON: I can't remember! I can't remember what to do – I'm not ready!

CAESAR: Ready or not. There's a baby coming.

NELSON: A baby! Oh, shit! Dad! There's gonna be blood! And afterbirth! And crying! And a baby! Needing things! From me! What have I got? I haven't even got A levels!

CAESAR: Nelson! Look at me. You've got me. I'm here with you, we're all here with you – your family, your friend and your wife. You're ready and everything is all gonna be alright. You're gonna take it all on one thing at a time – each thing you have to do in its time. And the first thing you have to do – is breathe.

NELSON breathes, KEISHA follows his lead.

Now tell your wife – it's gonna be alright.

NELSON: … It's gonna be alright…

KEISHA: … It's gonna be alright.

DEANNA: By the way – Yes.

CAESAR: 'Yes'?

DEANNA: Sorry, kids, I know we're busy, but, it's not every day someone asks me to marry them.

CAESAR: That's about to change.

CHE runs in with KEISHA's bag.

Right. Everybody. Ambulance.

CHE leads the way to the ambulance, KEISHA and NELSON follow, breathing. DEANNA and CAESAR are left looking at each other.

You ready?

DEANNA: As I'll ever be.

CAESAR: We're gonna be grandparents…

DEANNA takes his hand.

DEANNA: Breathe.

They breathe… They smile. They follow the kids towards the flashing blue light.

The end.